TREE HUNTING AND WALKING IN NORTH SOMERSET

Compiled by
John Shaw
1998 - 2004

Proceeds in aid of Bristol Children's Hospital
Registered charity number: 229945

Contents

1. Walk and drives in the car.

2. The trees have been measured roughly one yard up from the ground except for where the root base interferes in which case it would be higher. There are also stools and multi-trunks included as they could be ancient.

3. Over 2000 trees over l4ft in circumference, single trunk, multi trunk and old stools which could be ancient trees. Other large trees unable to measure due to water obstruction, see key below.

4. Children's Tree Quiz – Page 6 *(Answers Page 103)*

Key

P	Private ground - permission must be gained for entry/viewing
O	Open ground
M/T	Multi trunk
S/T	Single trunk
U/O	Undergrowth obstruction
W/O	Water obstruction
G/O	Ground obstruction
R/O	Rock obstruction
F/O	Fence obstruction
0/0	Crop obstruction
B/O	Branch obstruction
H/R	Hedgerow obstruction
T/O	Trunk obstruction
D/T	Decayed trunk
N/A	No access

O.S. Explorer Maps, 153.154.141 needsto be used in order to gain the full benefit of this book and to find the trees.

Published by Woodspring Resource Centre
Locking, Weston-super-Mare 01934 820800
ISBN 1 901 084 45 0

Introduction

This book is dedicated to the staff at the Bristol Children's Hospital as a way of saying thank you for the excellent care they took with my granddaughter who was a regular visitor to the hospital up until the age of 4. 100% of the proceeds made will go direct to the Children's Hospital. As for the copyright I am happy for any part of this book to be used for any purpose and would ask that should this happen then a small donation be made towards the Children's Hospital.

I thought I knew North Somerset extremely well, having been born at Locking and lived and worked here most of my life, until I started measuring large trees. When I first started I was expecting to find no more than 500 but in fact have ended up with just over 2000 trees and I'd like to thank the general public, landowners and farmers for their assistance in finding these trees. I have really enjoyed 'tree-hunting' and discovering places in North Somerset that I didn't even know existed.

The trees are numbered and registered in size and within parishes although I feel sure there are bound to be some that I have missed and therefore I have left space on page 104 to fill in if desired. There are also details of walks and car drives for all to enjoy in each parish with information of the large trees within the walk or drive. I have identified the trees by name although, again, some of these may be wrong.

I managed to get quite a few scratches and grazes whilst out and about and one time I very nearly fell in the river Avon at Easton in Gordano when measuring one tree, an oak 19'08 (ref. 834) which was right beside the river. I also saw much wildlife such as buzzards, cuckoos, deer, badgers, hares, rabbits, foxes and mink and one large adder, although I must say there was no trace of a black panther anywhere and I've been through just about every wood, hill, valley, river, road, drove, footpath and park in North Somerset. I also found some oxslips, orchids and pink/yellow primroses.

One of the best walks was in Upper Langford just after Christmas 2000, early one Sunday morning after it had snowed the night before. I was the first human to walk there after the snow and there were animal prints all over.

John Shaw

Large Trees of North Somerset

Pri/Open	No.	Size	Type	Location
P	162	30'01	Wellingtonia	Langford
O	347	30'00	Oak	Ashton Court
O	412	30'03	Oak	Ashton Court
P	2013	30'00	Sweet Chestnut	Leigh Woods
O	461	29'01	Oak	Ashton Court
O	541	29'07	Lime	Langford
O	1523	29'01	Lime	Long Ashton
O	1524	29'11	Lime	Long Ashton
O	158	28'01	Wellingtonia	Ashton Court
O	163	28'05	Oak	Ashton Court
O	397	28'01	Lime	Portishead
P	659	28'00	Wellingtonia	Failand
O	472	27'06	Yew	Abbots Leigh
O	588	27'00	Lime	Tickenham
P	705	27'03	Sycamore	Clapton in Gordano
P	776	27'03	Ash	Portbury
0	2057	27'00	Sweet Chestnut	Leigh Court
O	159	26'01	Wellingtonia	Ashton Court
P	254	26'06	Oak	Cleeve
P	164	26'02	Wellingtonia	Cleeve
P	898	26'04	Wellingtonia	Tyntesfield, Wraxall
O	1104	26'04	Field Maple	Priors Wood, Portbury
P	1365	26'07	Beech	Barrow Court
O	1754	26'00	Sycamore	Blagdon
0	2060	26'09	Sweet Chestnut	Leigh Court
O	160	25'11	Wellingtonia	Ashton Court
O	161	25'07	Wellingtonia	Ashton Court
P	258	25'00	Oak	Congresbury
O	542	25'04	Lime	Langford
P	567	25'03	Lime	Banwell
P	1009	25'06	Small Leaf Lime	Abbots Leigh
P	1015	25'00	Sweet Chestnut	Abbots Leigh
O	1152	25'06	Lime	Abbots Leigh
O	1273	25'00	Lime	Backwell
O	1819	25'07	Lime	Tickenham
O	2075	25'00	Lime	Abbots Leigh
P	2107	25'00	Cedar	Wrington

List of Parishes in North Somerset

* No trees over 14ft circumference found in Dundry, Kenn, Kewstoke, Kingston Seymour, Locking, Puxton or St. Georges.

Yew - Abbots Leigh Church Yard - Ref: 472 - 1400 years old

Twelve Trees to Find

1. A large Conker tree next to a school in a village.
    (Map ref: 154 66/44)
    _ _ _ _ _ _ _ _ _ _ _

2. A large Cedar on the old main road to Bristol
    in Long Ashton.
    _ _ _ _ _ _ _ _ _ _ _

3. The largest Yew in North Somerset in a
    Churchyard. *(Map ref: 154 74/54)*
    _ _ _ _ _ _ _ _ _ _ _

4. A spreading Oak in a car park near a boating
    lake. *(Map ref: 154 77/46)*
    _ _ _ _ _ _ _ _ _ _ _

5. A large Beech in a donkey field near
    Weston super Mare.
    _ _ _ _ _ _ _ _ _ _ _

6. This Wellingtonia is not a tree anymore and it
    is near to a set of traffic fights on a crossroads
    on the A38.
    _ _ _ _ _ _ _ _ _ _ _

7. This Willow is 80' tall and hollow on a bridlepath above

    B L – – D – N

8. This Wellingtonia is on an old railway bridge in the
    Parish of :–
    – A N D – – R D

9. This 26' plus single trunk Oak is in Cleeve and in Brockley

    B R – – K L – Y   – O O D –

10. The largest single trunk Holm Oak in North Somerset
    is in the wood above
    C – E – E D – N   C – U R –

11. 35 Wellingtonias together, all over 14'00.
    (Map ref: 154 70/52)
    _ _ _ _ _ _ _ _ _ _ _

12. 6 Wellingtonias threatened with the chain saw in
    a well know park estate.
    A S – T – –   C O – – T

Oak – Ref. 2103, 14'03
Dark Lane, Backwell

Wellingtonia– Ref. 141, 20'05
Skinners Lane, Churchill

Wellingtonia – Ref. 158, 28'01
Ashton Court – Under threat of being cut down

Abbots Leigh

Largest yew in North Somerset, 1400 years old, in the Churchyard, (ref. 472) at 27'06. Large unpollarded Sweet Chestnut, (ref. 593) at 19'04. Three small leaf Limes over 23ft plus with single trunk (ref. 1002, 1008 and 1009). Private Ground. Largest Sweet Chestnut (ref. 2013) 30'00 - split trunk. Magnificent Cedar 19'08 (ref. 459) and largest Horse Chestnut in North Somerset, 18'04 (ref. 480) in Church Road.

Largest Yew, pollarded Sweet Chestnut, unpollarded Sweet Chestnut, Small Leaf Lime, Cedar and Horse Chestnut are all in Abbots Leigh

Two Lucombe Oaks, Leigh Court House on front lawn, 17'04 (ref. 527) and 16'03 (ref. 524) Large single trunk Pine 16'08 (ref. 471) on main drive to Leigh Court House.

In The Car   See Easton in Gordano

On Foot   Leigh Woods - River Avon Walk - Fishpond Wood
Markham Brook - Suspension Bridge to Clifton Downs

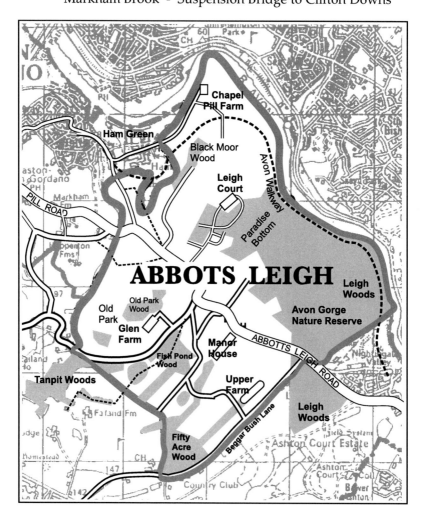

Abbots Leigh

Pri/Open	No.	Size	Feature	Type	Location	Map Ref.
O	472	27'06		Yew	Churchyard	74/54
P	478	23'09		Split Oak	Deerhurst, Church Road	"
P	476	21'00	*Pollard*	Oak	"	"
P	477	14'00	*Pollard*	Oak	"	"
P	459	19'08		Cedar	Abbots Leigh House	"
P	480	18'04		Horse Chestnut	"	"
P	481	16'01		Oak	Field below Abbots Leigh House	73/54
P	482	17'04	*M/T*	Oak	"	"
P	479	16'05	*Pollard*	Oak	Long Barn, Church Road	74/54
P	473	14'04	*Pollard*	Oak	63 Church Road	"
P	474	16'03	*Pollard*	Oak	"	"
P	475	15'00	*Pollard*	Oak	"	"
P	589	15'01	*Pollard*	Oak	Field, Bosley, Sandy Lane	73/54
P	590	14'01	*Pollard*	Oak	"	"
P	588	16'07	*Pollard*	Oak	"	"
O	591	U/O	*Pollard*	Oak	Next to spring, Sandy Lane	"
O	592	U/O	*Pollard*	Oak	"	"
O	593	19'04		Sweet Chestnut	100 yards from spring, Sandy Lane	"
O	657	15'01		Beech	Off Tanpit Wood, Sandy Lane	"
O	658		*M/T*	Willow	Near Mulberry Farm, Sandy Lane	"
O	666	14'10	*4 trunks*	Lime	Markham Brook, south west A369	74/52
O	667	14'03	*3 trunks*	Ash	"	"
O	668	14'02	*4 trunks*	Lime	"	"
O	665	15'09	*4 trunks*	Lime	"	"
O	594	14'06	*3 trunks*	Sweet Chestnut	Fish Pond Wood, top part	73/53
O	595	M/T	*Old stool 9 trunks*	Sweet Chestnut	"	"
O	596	16'10	*4 trunks*	Sweet Chestnut	"	"
O	597	14'03	*Very tall*	Beech	Fish Pond Wood, near orchard	"
O	599	15'02		Beech	Fish Pond Wood, stream	"
O	598	14'00		Sycamore	Fish Pond Wood, fishpond	"
O	653	14'03		Sweet Chestnut	Fish Pond Wood, behind log barn	"
P	1007	23'02	*S/T*	Small Leaf)	Lime Field, part of Glen Farm	"
P	1008	23'00		Small Leaf Lime)	*1007, 1008, 1009, 1010 - three very*	"
P	1009	25'06	*Old*	Small Leaf Lime)	*large single trunk small leaf limes*	"
P	1010	16'07	*Pollard*	Sweet Chestnut)	*and one very old Sweet Chestnut*	"
P	1011	14'08		Oak	Field, part of Glen Farm	"
P	1012	16'09		Oak	"	"
P	1013	18'09		Oak	"	"
P	1012	16'09		Oak	"	"
P	1013	18'09		Oak	"	"
P	1014	15'10		Oak	"	"

Abbots Leigh

Pri/Open	No.	Size	Feature	Type	Location	Map Ref.
P	1015	25'00		Sweet Chestnut	Field, part of Glen Farm	73/53
P	1016	18'08	*Pollard*	Oak	Field, North of Old Park Wood	"
P	1017	14'01	*Pollard*	Sycamore	Top of Old Park Wood	"
P	1018	M/T	*4 trunks*	Sweet Chestnut	Bottom of Old Park Wood	"
P	1019	M/T	*6 trunks*	Lime	Old Park Wood, near stream	"
P	1020	M/T	*6 trunks*	Lime	"	"
P	1021	18'03	*M/T, stool*	Sycamore	"	"
P	1022	M/T	*5 trunks*	Sycamore	"	"
P	1023	M/T	*8 trunks*	Sycamore	"	"

Many thanks to Jan Wakeham

Abbots Leigh Parish,   Leigh Woods, Paradise Bottom

Pri/Open	No.	Size	Feature	Type	Location	Map Ref.
O	2043	M/T	*Stool*	Sweet Chestnut	Sloops South Side	74/54
O	2044	"	"		"	"
O	2045	"	"		"	"
O	2046	"	"		"	"
O	2047	"	"		"	"
O	2048	"	"		"	"
O	2049	"	"		"	"
O	2050	"	"		"	"
O	2051	"	"		"	"
O	2052	"	"		"	"
O	2053	"	"		"	"
O	2054	"	"		"	"
O	2055	"	"	Lime	"	"
O	2056	"	"	Lime	"	"
O	2057	27'00	*Stool, M/T*	Sweet Chestnut	"	"
O	2058	21'09	*Stool, M/T*		"	"
O	2059	17'07	*Single trunk*		"	"
O	2065	M/T		Ash	Outcrop right of Seventh Quarry	74/55
O	2066	M/T		Lime	Below Seventh Quarry	"
O	2067	14'10		Lime	"	"
O	2068	M/T		Lime	Between Fifth and Sixth Quarry	
O	2069	M/T		Lime	"	"
O	2070	M/T		Lime	"	"
O	2071	M/T		Lime	"	"
O	2072	M/T		Lime	Above Fifth Quarry	
O	2073	M/T		Lime	"	"
O	2074	M/T	*Collapsed*	Lime	Left side Fifth Quarry	74/55
O	2075	25'00	*Single stump*	Lime	Outcrop 100 yards below fence right side Fourth Quarry	"
O	2076	M/T	*9 trunks*	Lime	Near Purple Trail - parish wall	73/55
O	2077	17'05	*Single trunk*	Yew	Gap in parish wall 'Yew of Yore'	"

Abbots Leigh Parish

Leigh Woods, Above Road, Car Park to Locked Gate

Pri/Open	No.	Size	Feature	Type	Location	Map Ref.
O	2003	M/T		Lime	Car park wood	74.75 / 54.55
O	2004	M/T		Lime	"	"
O	2005	M/T		Lime	"	"
O	2006	M/T		Lime	"	"
O	2007	14'02	3 trunk	Yew	"	"
O	2008	23'06	8 trunk	Lime	Gulley above road	"
O	2009	16'00	Split	Oak	Next to gate	"
O	2010	16'02	9 trunk	Lime	"	"
P	2011	18'06	6 trunk, stool	Sweet Chestnut		"
P	2012	18'06	Single trunk	Sweet Chestnut	* 30' root base, 18'6" at 30' high	"
P	2013	30'00	Split trunk	Sweet Chestnut	* 40' root base, nearly dead	"
P	2014	24'03	Stool	Sweet Chestnut		"
P	2015	15'02		Oak		"
P	2016	21'09		Sweet Chestnut		"
P	2017	16'04		Sweet Chestnut		"
P	2018	20'00		Sweet Chestnut		"
P	2019	20'05		Sweet Chestnut		"
P	2020	15'08		Oak		"
P	2021	N/A		Sweet Chestnut		"
P	2022 - 2041			Sweet Chestnuts	Oak Wood	"

Abbots Leigh Parish,

Leigh Court Area

Pri/Open	No.	Size	Feature	Type	Location	Map Ref.
O	543	20'06		Cedar	Front lawn, Leigh Court	74/54
O	519	19'08		Wellingtonia		
O	522	18'08	7' stump, one shoot growing	Sweet Chestnut	"	"
O	527	17'04		Lucombe Oak	"	"
O	524	16'03		Lucombe Oak	"	"
O	526	M/T	7 trunks	Lime	"	"
O	521	U/O		Lime	"	"
O	523	U/O		Lime	"	"
O	1136	15'08		Holm Oak	Main car park woods, Leigh Court	"
O	519	19'08		Wellingtonia	"	"
O	532	17'07		Sweet Chestnut	"	"
O	533	17'06	Cut down Spring 2000	Wellington	"	"
O	534	17'07		Wellingtonia	"	"
O	471	16'08		Pine	"	"
O	520	14'00		Oak	Next to car park, Leigh Court	"
O	535	14'10		Sweet Chestnut	"	"
O	1137	17'11		Sweet Chestnut	"	"

Abbots   Leigh Parish,   Leigh Court Area

Pri/Open	No.	Size	Feature	Type	Location	Map Ref.
O	1138	14'07		Sweet Chestnut	"	"
O	1139	M/T		Lime	"	"
O	1140	M/T		Lime	"	"
					Paradise Bottom	
O	1141	M/T		Lime	Footpath towards railway bridge	74/75/54
O	1142	M/T		Lime	"	"
O	1140	M/T		Lime	"	"
O	1144	M/T		Lime	Footpath towards railway bridge	"
O	1145	M/T		Lime	"	"
O	1146	M/T		Lime	"	"
O	1147	M/T		Lime	"	"
O	1148	M/T		Lime	"	"
O	1149	M/T		Lime	"	"
O	1150	M/T		Lime	"	"
O	1151	23'01	6 trunks	Lime	Near ditch	"
O	1152	25'06	7 trunks	Lime	Near ditch	"
O	1153	18'05	Single trunk	Lime	By railway bridge	"
O	1154	18'06	Pollard	Sweet Chestnut		"
O	1155	20'00	10 trunks	Lime	Next to pond	74/75/54
O	1156	23'01	23'1 at 15'	Sweet Chestnut	Near pond	"
X	1157	X	Huge trunk		Fallen Over	"
O	1158	18'08		Oak	Near pond	"
O	1159	24'08		Wellingtonia	Near pond	"
0	1160	18'08		Lime	Entrance in by house	"

Abbots Leigh   Old Oak Park

Pri/Open	No.	Size	Feature	Type	Location	Map Ref.
P	875	18'10	7Small branches	Oak	Field South of railway	75/53
P	836	15'03	Split trunk	Ash	Railway embankment	"
P	837	17'00		Oak	By pond, North of railway	"
P	838	19'10		Oak	"	"
P	839	14'01		Oak	"	"
P	840	14'03		Oak	"	"
P	841	18'07		Oak	Pond, field	"
P	842	19'00		Oak	Pond stream, South of railway	"
P	843	19'01		Oak	Field, top, South of railway	"
P	844	14'07		Oak	Field edge, South of railway	"
P	845	16'07		Oak	Field, South of railway	"
P	846	14'02		Oak	"	"
P	847	15'05		Oak	Black Moor Wood, very top	"

❑ ❑ ❑ ❑ ❑

Backwell

There are 7 various trees over 14'00 around Backwell House and a very large Wellingtonia at 21'05 (ref. 149) in Church Lane. 21'00 Lime, (ref. 1273) in Backwell Hill woods and another six over 14'00. Two 25'00 plus single trunk Limes (ref. 1401 and 1402) on edge of Bourton Coombe are in desperate need of topping.

In The Car   Backwell - Lulsgate - Winford - Regil - Barrow Gurney
              Nempnett Thrubwell - Compton Martin - Bishop Sutton
              Chelswood - Chew Magna - Winford - Lulsgate
              Brockley Coombe - Redhill - Wrington - Cleeve - Backwell

On Foot   Public Footpaths -   Backwell Common   White Oak House
                                    Bourton Combe   Wrington Warren

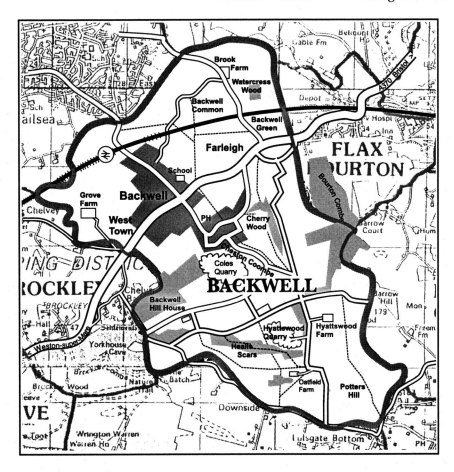

Take the children, grandchildren or grandparents to Backwell Lake
to feed the ducks and, perhaps, enjoy an ice cream.

Backwell

Pri/Open	No.	Size	Feature	Type	Location	Map Ref.
P	149	21'05		Wellingtonia	Church Lane	68/45
P	1	14'03		Beech	"	"
P	34	M/T		Cypress	"	"
P	537	16'02		Oak	Near dry ditch North of railway line	68/50
P	540	15'05		Oak	Next to old drove South of railway line	
P	538	14'00		Oak	"	"
P	539	U/O		Oak	"	"
P	275	17'05		Lime	Backwell House	"
P	277	16'02		Oak	"	"
P	279	16'10		Oak	"	"
P	280	15'02		Beech	"	"
P	236	14'09		Horse Chestnut	"	"
P	278	14'00		Lime	"	"
P	281	14'00		Horse Chestnut	"	"
O	1354	14'11	Small leaf	Lime	Backwell Down House, P. Footpath	68/49
O	1355	20'00	Only half a trunk left	Lime	"	"
O	1356	14'00		Sycamore	"	"
P	1357	14'01		Ash	Backwell Down House, field	"
P	1358	14'00		Lime	"	"
O	1359	M/T	6 trunks	Ash	Cherry Wood	
O	1360	F/O	Gnarled	Ash	Jubilee Stone field, lower	67/49
O	1361	14'03	Stumpy	Lime	"	"
P	1920	W/O	Fallen over	Oak	Watercress Wood	70/49
P	1921	15'6	Split	Oak	Next to brook	"
P	1922	M/T		Alder	"	"
O	1367	14'00		Yew	Bourton Combe Woods, top half	68/50 "
O	1368	M/T		Yew	"	"
O	1369	15'00	Initials - RS 1958 JS	Beech	"	"
					"	"
P	1397	17'00		Beech	Stancombe Quarry Woods	68/50
P	1398	15'04		Beech	"	"
P	1399		Decayed trunk	Ash	Old path below Keepers Cottage	"
P	1400		Coppiced	Hazel	"	"
P	1401	21'00	30'+ at 10'	Lime	Stancombe Quarry	"
P	1402	21'00	Top half	Lime	(Two of the largest Limes	"
P	1403		collapsed	Lime	in North Somerset)	"
O	1413	16'02		Yew	Cheston Coombe West	67/49
O	1414	15'10		Yew	"	"
O	1415	15'08		Yew	"	"
O	1416	14'09		Yew	Cheston Coombe East (No small children - open cliffs)	67/49
O	1417	M/T		Ash	Heals Scars	66/49
O	1418		Decayed trunk	Ash	Public foot path, Coombe Head Farm	"

Backwell

Pri/Open	No.	Size	Feature	Type	Location	Map Ref.
P	1419	N/A		Holm Oak	Robinson Way	66/48
P	1927	15'05		Oak	Next to Grove Farm	68/48
P	1928	19'00		Oak	" Hedgerow	"
0	1929	19'10	Dead, hollow Owls in trunk	Oak	" Field	"
P	1933	16'03	Metal bar	Oak	Field North Grove Farm, on a ridge	"

Backwell

Backwell Hill House Woods

Pri/Open	No.	Size	Feature	Type	Location	Map Ref.
P	1337	14'10		Beech	Backwell Hill House	"
P	1338	14'04		Beech	"	"
P	1339	15'02		Beech	"	"
P	260	15'04		Holm Oak	"	"
P	259	14'11		Holm Oak	"	"
P	1340	M/T		Beech	"	"
O	1282	21'09	Stool	Lime	Near quarry lower	67/48
O	1281	15'08		Lime	"	"
O	1276	M/T	Stool	Ash	Next to orchard below woods	"
O	1275	15'03		Yew	Middle wood, parish boundary	"
O	1331	20'02		Lime	Above reservoir	"
O	1332	M/T		Lime	"	"
O	1333	M/T		Lime	"	"
O	1334	16'10		Lime	"	"
O	1280	14'00	Pollard	Oak	Lower wood	"
O	1265	M/T	20' plus	Lime	Lower wood, parish boundary	"
O	1266	16'04		Lime		
O	1267	M/T		Lime		
O	1268	M/T		Lime		
O	1269	M/T		Lime		
O	1270	M/T		Lime		
O	1271	M/T		Lime		
O	1272	M/T		Lime		
O	1273	25'00	Growing on wall	Lime		
O	1274	M/T				
O	1277	M/T		Lime		
O	1278	16'07		Lime		
O	1279	15'07		Lime		

Trees, ref. 1265 - 1274 & 1277 - 1279, all to be found at Lower wood, parish boundary.

Oak – Ref: 2103
Top of Dark Lane, near to ➤
Backwell Junior School

Banwell

Mr Parsons of Banwell Castle gave me some information regarding large limes in Banwell Wood. I found an extremely large single trunk lime, 25'3 (ref. 567) and also two others which I was unable to measure due to undergrowth obstruction. These were both well over 20' (ref. 569 and 571). This is private property and permission for access must be gained.

Banwell Abbey

There is a Wellingtonia at 20'01 (ref. 138) which has been damaged both by a German bomb and lightning but is still growing. Many thanks to Mrs Dawson for this information. This is private property and permission must be gained for access.

Towerhead House

There is a magnificent 17'10 plane (ref. 801) plus an unusual fern beech at 12'10 (not numbered as it is under 14'00) in the grounds of this house. Only 3 other fern beech that I could find in North Somerset. There is a 19'00 very large oak (ref. 803), not pollarded, in the field next to the house. This is private ground.

The Caves, Banwell Hill

12 trees over 14'00 of which there is a magnificent beech with the names of Angie and Dean carved into and is 16'04 (ref. 90). These trees were planted by Bishop Lawes. Many thanks to John Haines for this information. Private property.

In The Car	Banwell - Christon
	Loxton - Compton Bishop
	Axbridge Town Centre
	Shipham Lane
	Winscombe - Banwell

On Foot Public Footpaths
Bell Inn (good Pint)
public footpath off
High Street to Banwell Hill

Banwell Castle to
Compton Bishop

Banwell Castle to
Winscombe Church
Banwell Church is well
worth a look

Many thanks to John Haines, Mrs Dawson and Mr Parsons

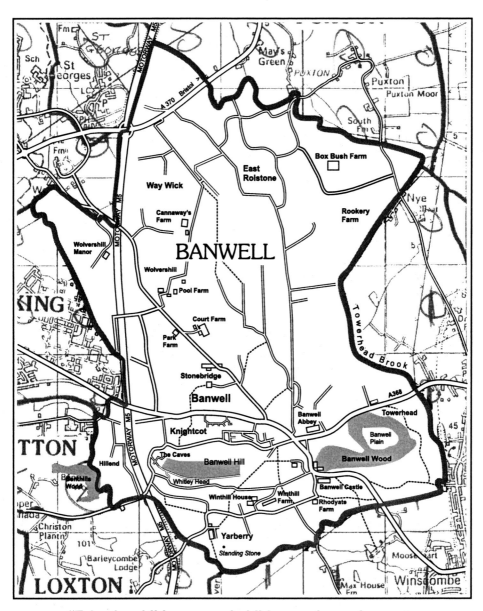

*"Take the children, grand-children and grand-parents
paddling in the River Banwell at Riverside"*

*'Banwell Tower - Outstanding views (limited opening hours)
'Banwell Caves' - (limited opening hours) Both worth a visit*

Wellingtonia - 20'00 Ref: 138
◄ *Banwell Abbey*
Struck by German Bomb and by Lightning

Banwell

Pri/Open	No.	Size	Feature	Type	Location	Map Ref.
P	567	25'03	*Single trunk*	Lime	Banwell Woods, South	58/40
					(no public access)	
P	570	180'6	*Single trunk*	Lime	"	"
P	103	17'05	*Single trunk*	Lime	"	"
P	569	M/T		Lime	"	"
P	571	M/T		Lime	"	"
P	568	14'04		Ash	Banwell Woods, near green metal	"
P	804	15'00	*S/T*	Lime	Banwell Woods, North	"
P	800	15'02	*Pollard, M/T*	Willow	Moor Road small holding	59/39
P	801	17'10		Plane	Towerhead House, grounds	59/41
P	802	14'00		Horse Chestnut	Towerhead House, field *(struckby lightening in July 2001)*	"
P	803	19'00		Oak	Towerhead House, hedgerow	"
P	x	12'10	*Rare*	Fern Beech	Towerhead House, grounds	"
P	149	21'05		Wellingtonia	Banwell Abbey *(no public access)*	59/40
P	138	20'01		Wellingtonia	Banwell Abbey *(damaged by German bombs and lightning)*	"
P	120	18'10		Wellingtonia	Banwell Abbey	"
P	49	15'06		Wellingtonia	"	"
P	4	14'03		Horse Chestnut	"	"
P	5	14'06		Turkey Holm Oak	"	"
P	117	18'08		Wellingtonia	Dark Lane	"
P	118	18'07		Wellingtonia	"	"
P	119	18'03		Wellingtonia	"	"
P	72	16'08		Cedar	"	"
O	688	17'09		Beech	Farm trail to Banwell Hill	58/39
0	696	14'01		Beech	"	"
O	691	15'04		Beech	Farm trail to Banwell Hill	58/39
P	692	15'11	*5 trunks*	Beech	Farm outbuildings, South WhitleyHead	"
P	693	15'10		Beech	The Caves, Banwell Hill	58/38
P	694	15'01		Beech	"	"
P	697	14'09		Beech	"	"
P	698	14'10		Oak	"	"
P	699	14'09		Copper Beech	"	"
P	695	15'05	*5 trunks*	Beech	Near metal tank	"
P	689	16'02	*2 trunks*	Beech	Near Folly Tower	"
P	690	16'04		Beech	"	"
O	1980	U/O	*Pollard*	Oak	Parish boundary, bank north of Max House Farm, public footpath, pylon in field	58/40

Barrow Gurney

Two beautiful Cedars at Barrow Court in excellent condition. One is 16'06 (ref. 249) and the other is 16'01 (ref. 250). Six old pollarded Oaks, all over 14'00 around Barrow Court.

By far the largest Beech in North Somerset, 26'07 split trunk (ref. 1365) in a field above Barrow Court. 19'00 Oak on public footpath, north side of Slade Wood (ref. 1712)

In The Car   Barrow Gurney - Winford - Chew Magna - Chew Stoke

Regil - Winford Manor - Felton - Barrow Gurney

On Foot   Public footpaths :-   Jubilee Stone   -   Dundry

Monarchs Way   -   Flax Bourton

Barrow Gurney to Barrow Hill Wood on to Water Catch Farm and down the hill to the Conygar and Bourton Combe

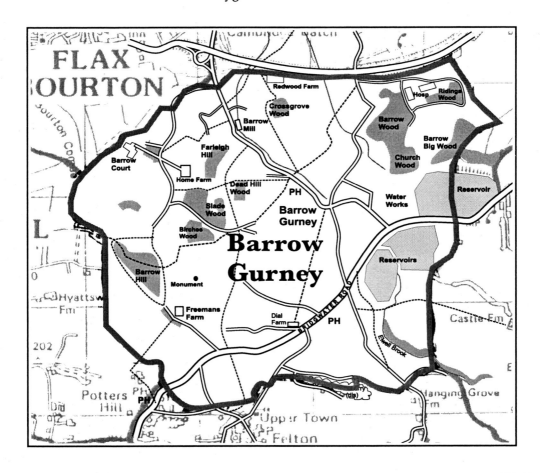

Barrow Gurney

Pri/Open	No.	Size	Feature	Type	Location	Map Ref.
O	246	16'9		Oak	Hedgerow next to Barrow Lane	68/52
O	245	U/O		Oak	"	"
P	1581	18'9	*25' at 10'*	Oak	Barrow Hospital, field, right hand right hand side entrance	69/53
P	1582	14'00		Oak	Barrow Hospital, left side, main entrance	"
P	1583	F/O		Willow	Barrow Hospital, staff houses	"
P	1584	15'02		Oak	Barrow Hospital, Hay shed	"
P	671	U/O		Oak	Next to spring wild country wild country hedgerow	68/53
P	669	1/4	*4 trunks*	Oak	Church Wood near stone bridge	"
P	670	16'03		Oak	Barrow Big Wood, North left edge	"
P	672	14'01		Oak	Wild country hedgerow near Hospital	"
O	1421	14'06	*Next to wall*	Yew	The Conygar Woods	68/50
O	1585	14'00	*80' +*	Oak	Barrow woods	68/53
O	1586	M/T	*6 trunk stool*	Ash	"	"
O	1557	15'07	*80' +*	Oak	"	"
O	1588	16'07	*M/T, base measure*	Ash	"	"
O	1589	17'01	*Split*	Ash	Barrow woods, near orchard	"
				Barrow Court		
P	249	16'06		Cedar	Barrow Court, Grounds	68/51
P	250	15'01		Cedar	"	"
P	248	14'01		Horse Chestnut	"	"
P	247	15'07		Horse Chestnut	"	"
P	1362	15'10		Beech	Field above Barrow Court	
P	1363	17'08	*Stump dead*	Beech	"	"
P	1364	17'06		Beech	"	"
P	1365	26'07	*Split trunk 1st trunk 18'10 2nd trunk 13'03*	Beech	" *Largest Beech in North Somerset*	"
P	1366	16'07	*Rabbit warren*	Beech	"	"
P	1590	M/T		Willow	Barrow Dogs Home, Barrow Wood brook	68/53 "
P	1591	"		Willow	"	"
O	2106	"		Bay	Monarchs Way	68/54
O	1496	17'02	*M/T, base measure*	Sycamore	Barrow Hill Lane	67/51
O	1497	M/T		Sycamore	"	"
O	1498	"	*4 trunk, nettle bed*	Ash	Barrow Hill, public footpath to Park Cottage	"
O	1499	"	*Layered, nettle bed*	Ash	Barrow Hill, public footpath to Park Cottage	"

Barrow Gurney

Pri/Open	No.	Size	Feature	Type	Location	Map Ref.
O	1500	15'08	*M/T, stool*	Ash	Barrow Hill, Jubilee Stone field	67/51
O	1501	14'04	*Bulbous base*	Ash	West of Yew Tree Farm, public f/p	66/51
O	1527	U/O		Ash	Public footpath near Batches Wood H/R	67/52
O	1528	16'03		Oak	H/R Batches Wood, bridle path	"
O	1529	14'07	*Next to Hawthorn*	Oak	Batches Wood, field	"
O	1530	14'00	*Covered in Ivy*	Ash	Naish Lane, ancient bank	"
P	1531	U/O	*80 + tall*	Ash	Road to Stevens' Farm	"
P	1532	17'09	*Not pollard, huge*	Oak	Near Stevens Farm woods	"
P	1533	14'00	*Not pollard,*	Oak	"	"
P	1534	U/O		Oak	H/R top of Slade Lane	"
O	1712	19'	*Huge, not pollard*	Oak	Public foot path, north of Slade Wood	67/52
O	1713	15'10	*Single trunk*	Ash	Public foot path, west of Deadhill Wood	68/52
O	1714	15'08		Oak	"	"
O	1715	16'08		Oak	Public foot path, east o Slade Wood	67/52
P	1716	14'00	*80 + tall*	Oak	Slade Wood	"
P	1562	W/O	*M/T*	Ash	Barrow Mill stream	68/52
P	1563	"	*M/T*	Ash	"	"
P	1564	"	*M/T*	Alder	"	"
P	1565	"	*M/T*	Aider	Barrow Mill Stream	"
P	1566	"	*M/T*	Alder	"	"
P	1567	"	*M/T*	Willow	"	"
P	1568	M/T	*Stool*	Ash	Cosgrove Wood	"
P	1569	"	*Stool*	Ash	"	"
P	1570	"	*Stool*	Ash	"	"
P	1571	"	*Stool*	Ash	"	"
P	1572	"	*Stool*	Ash	"	"
P	1573	"	*Stool*	Ash	"	"
P	1574	"	*Stool*	Ash	"	"
P	1575	"		Ash	Bank, near Cosgrove Wood	"
P	1576	16'07	*80' +,sharp Dog Rose*	Oak	Barrow Wood Brook	"
P	1577	15'05	*Spreading*	Oak	"	"
P	1578	M/T	*With plum tree*	Ash	"	"
P	1579	F/O	*Lost large branch*	Oak	"	"
P	1580	16'03		Oak	Old ditch, Redwood Farm, 200 yards east	69/52

❑ ❑ ❑ ❑ ❑

Blagdon

Extremely large Willow (ref. 1545), unable to measure due to water obstruction, tree has collapsed across river. Tremendous amount of large Alders on the river which have been pollarded over the years.

Coombe Lodge   There is a huge single trunk lime 24'03 (ref. 271) and four large beech trees over 15' and a 17'10 wellingtonia (ref. 463) in the woods. Many thanks to John Bowden for his assistance. Private property.

Pump Rooms,   A large wellingtonia 20'07 and three magnificent cedars in the
Blagdon Lake   grounds.

In The Car   Blagdon - Charterhouse - Cheddar Gorge - Shipham Tynings Farm - Charterhouse - Blagdon

On Foot   Blagdon Lake - Limestone Link - Aldwick Court Langford Inn (good food)

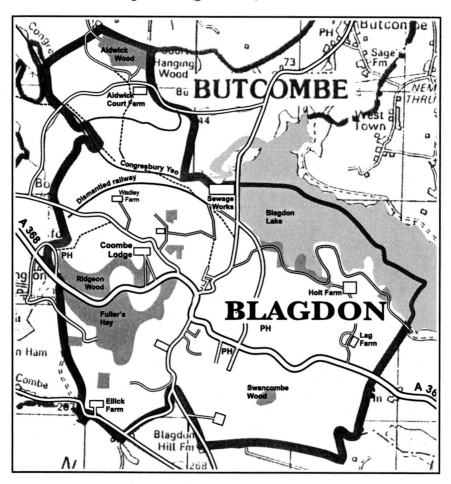

Aldwick   There is a 20'04 oak (ref. 144) in a field next to the post box. This, along with the other large pollarded oaks would have been a park for Aldwick Court. There are another 17 trees of which 14 are oaks and 3 are Beech around Aldwick Court. Most of these can be seen from the road. This is private property and permission must be gained for access.

In The Car   Butcombe - Nempnett Thrubwell - Winford
Wrington - Blagdon and onto the Mendips.

On Foot   Public foot paths Blagdon Lake - Two Rivers Way - Havyatt Green

Many thanks to: Mrs Mead, Blagdon Court, John Bawden, Coombe Lodge

Blagdon Parish   Aldwick

Pri/Open	No.	Size	Feature	Type	Location	Map Ref.
P	144	20'04	*20' High trunk at 20'*	Oak	Field next to Post Box	61/49
P	105	17'09		Oak	"	"
P	875	14'08		Oak	Field by SWEB pole	"
P	876	15'10		Oak	"	"
P	877	16'07		Oak	Aldwick Wood	"
P	878	14'00		Oak	Aldwick Court	"
P	879	14'09		Oak	Aldwick Court, orchard	"
P	880	15'07		Oak	"	"
P	881	14'08		Oak	"	"
P	882	14'09		Oak	Aldwick Court, driveway	"
P	883	18'04		Beech	Field, left of main drive, Aldwick Court	"
P	884	14'09		Beech	Field below Aldwick Court	"
P	885	15'09		Beech	"	"
O	886	14'00		Oak	Road next to East Cottage	"
O	887	U/O		Oak	"	"
O	888	15'06		Oak	Aldwick Court, near stream	"
P	889	17'04		Oak	Aldwick Court, field next to stream	"
P	890	16'00		Oak	"	"
P	1471	W/O		Oak	Pond, left of woodlands	"

A large Cedar tree fell down and hit Coombe Lodge — it is now part of the bar at Blagdon Village Hall

**'Take the children and grandparents paddling in the
ford below the Plume of Feathers pub'**

Blagdon

Pri/Open	No.	Size	Feature	Type	Location	Map Ref.
O	246	16'09		Oak	Hedgerow next to Barrow Lane	68/52
P	271	24'03		Lime	Coombe Lodge area	59/49
P	463	17'10		Wellingtonia	"	"
P	269	16'02		Beech	"	"
P	464	16'07		Beech	"	"
P	267	15'01		Beech	"	"
P	268	15'11		Beech	"	"
P	274	15'03		Cedar	"	"
P	273	16'07		Sweet Chestnut	"	"
P	272	16'05		Oak	"	"
P	270	14'04		Lime	"	"
P	143	20'07		Wellingtonia	Blagdon Water Works	59/50
P	104	17'02		Cedar	"	"
P	59	15'03		Cedar	"	"
P	60	15'04		Wellingtonia	"	"
P	125	18'09		Oak	"	"
P	84	16'10		Oak	Field, Dark Lane	"
P	85	16'00		Oak	"	"
O	465	18'01		Oak	A368 Blagdon to Ubley	59/51
P	17	14'06	*X XX*	Beech	Blagdon Court	59/50
O	1535	W/O		Alder	River Yeo area, Emley Lane to Blagdon Lake	60/49/50 "
O	1536	W/O		Alder	"	"
O	1537	W/O		Alder	"	"
P	1538	W/O		Alder	"	"
O	1539	W/O		Aider	"	"
O	1540	W/O		Alder	"	"
O	1541	W/O		Alder	"	"
O	1542	W/O		Alder	"	"
O	1543	W/O		Alder	"	"
O	1544	18'07		Alder	"	"
O	1545	W/O		Willow	River Yeo area, Emley Lane *Largest in North Somerset, collapsed across river*	60/49/50
O	1546	W/O		Oak	"	"
O	1547	W/O		Oak	"	"
O	1548	W/O		Oak	"	"
O	1549	W/O	*Very large*	Ash	"	"
O	1550	14'00	*Stone post*	Oak	" hedgerow	"

"Uxford Bridge on the public footpath across the Yeo is made up of three large stones, 8' x 4' x 1'
– How did they get there?"

"See the Spring Flowers at Coombe Lodge"

Blagdon

Pri/Open	No.	Size	Feature	Type	Location	Map Ref.
O	1551	16'04		Oak	River Yeo Area, Emley Lane	60/48/49
O	1653	W/O		Alder	River Yeo Area, Emley Lane to Wrington Parish Boundary	61/48/49
O	1654	W/O		Alder	"	"
O	1655	W/O		Alder	"	"
O	1656	W/O		Alder	"	"
O	1657	W/O		Alder	"	"
O	1658	W/O		Alder	"	"
O	1659	W/O		Alder	"	"
O	1660	W/O		Aider	"	"
O	1661	W/O		Alder	"	"
O	1662	W/O		Alder	"	"
O	1663	W/O		Alder	"	"
O	1664	W/O			*Collapsed across Willow river*	"
O	1665	W/O	*Laying in river*	Oak	"	"
O	1666	14'06		Oak	Field near river	"
P	1738	19'00	*Pollard*	Oak	Near public foot path, field Old Farm	59/49
O	1739	15'00	*Covered in ivy*	Lime	Public foot path, wood east of the park	"
P	1740	M/T	*7 trunks*	Ash	Ellick Road gully	58/50
P	1741	15'03		Beech	Swancoombe Wood	"
P	1742	U/O	*Pollard*	Oak	Small wood east of Swancoombe Wood	"
O	1743	U/O		Oak	Public foot path, ancient drove east end to Milk Factory	59/50/51
O	1744	U/O		Oak	"	"
O	1745	U/O		Oak	"	"
O	1746	18'00	*Next to gate*	Oak	"	"
O	1747	U/O		Ash	"	"
O	1748	U/O	*Stile*	Oak	Public foot path, ancient drove east end to Blagdon Lake	59/50/51
P	1749	N/A		Oak	Milk Factory group	58/60
P	1750	W/O		Oak	Holt Farm spring	59/60
P	1751	W/O		Oak	"	"
P	1752	W/O		Oak	"	"
P	1753	W/O		Oak	Holt Farm pond	59/60
O	1754	26'00	*Large trunk, small tree*	Sycamore	Public foot path, Live & Let Live pub	58/50
P	1764	16'02	*Pot bellied, layered, 12 trunks*	Ash	Field east of Mercombe Wood	58/51
O	2094	16'06		Lime	FP below Leaze Farm	

X   *Quite a few large Beech trees were lost in the great storm in the eighties.*
XX   *Was this the old packhorse route next to Blagdon Court and on to Blagdon Church.*

Bleadon

There is a 15'06 (ref. 763) 80'00 tall hollow willow on the bridle path. How it is managing to still be standing being so close to the sea I do not know.   There is also a very large walnut tree (no ref. - not over 14'00).

In The Car Roman Road (good views) - Bleadon - Loxton - Cross

Axbndge Town Centre - Cheddar Gorge - Mendip Hills

On Foot West Mendip Way to Loxton - Banwell Caves - Hutton

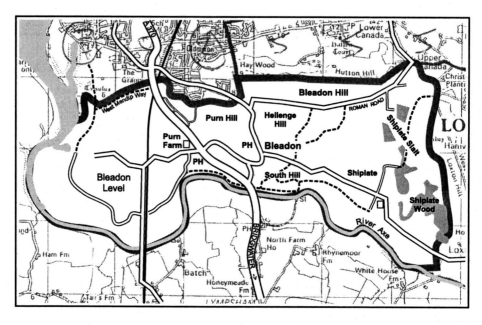

Bleadon

Pri/Open	No.	Size	Feature	Type	Location	Map Ref.
P	763	15'06	*Pollard* *80' tall, hollow*	Willow	Bridlepath, boundary with Hutton	58/30
					Shiplate Wood	
P	1481	14'00	*M/T*	Ash	Left side tractor track	57/35
P	1482	14'02		Oak	"	"
P	1483	M/T	*Triple*	Ash	Left side valley lower	"
P	1484	M/T	*Split*	Ash	"	"
P	1485	M/T	*4 trunks*	Ash	"	"

Brockley

Brockley Fields Above A370

14 trees over 14'00. The large cedar (ref. 133) at 19'02 has had quite a bit of wind damage and is the 3rd largest cedar in North Somerset. These fields would have been part of Brockley Hall many years ago. This is private ground but does have a public footpath running through it.

Brockley Hall

Two magnificent cedar trees in excellent condition, 17'00 (ref. 186) and 16'02 (ref. 188). There is also a 15'10 (ref. 190) copper beech in Geoff Hobbs garden. This is very large for a copper beech. This is private ground but the trees can be seen from the road.

Brockley Woods

12 trees over 14'00. There is also a large beech, 16'02 (ref. 262) which was cut down in Spring 2001.

In The Car

Brockley to Butcombe
Butcombe to Blagdon
Blagdon to Wrington
Wrington Hill to Cleeve
Cleeve to Brockley

On Foot

Wrington Warren
Church Town
Goblin Combe
Nailsea West End

"Walk from traffic lights at Brockley Combe on the old carriageway and imagine what it was like all those years ago on the Old Bowling Green, still there covered in trees."

Many thanks to Geoff Hobbs

Cedar – Ref. 133, 19'02
Over wall near traffic lights ➤
at Brockley Coombe

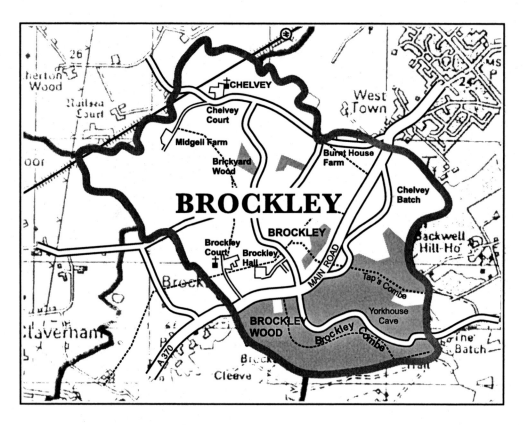

Brockley

Pri/Open	No.	Size	Feature	Type	Location	Map Ref.
P	133	19'02		Cedar	Brockley fields, South of A370	67/47
P	122	18'00	*Pollard*	Oak	"	"
P	99	17'01	*Pollard*	Oak	"	"
P	100	17'01		Lime	"	"
P	75	16'00	*Pollard*	Oak	"	"
P	76	16'00		Oak	"	"
P	51	15'03		Lime	"	"
P	52	15'05	*Pollard*	Oak	"	"
P	53	15'09		Plane	"	"
P	54	15'00		Lime	"	"
P	10	14'03		Lime	"	"
P	11	14'04		Lime	"	"
P	12	14'09	*Pollard*	Oak	"	"
P	13	14'11		Sweet Chestnut	"	"
P	186	17'00		Cedar	Brockley Hall	"
P	188	16'02		Cedar	"	"
P	190	15'10		Copper Beech	"	"

Brockley   (North or Above A370)

Pri/Open	No.	Size	Feature	Type	Location	Map Ref.
O	381	19'11		Oak	Near A370	67/47
O	385	17'00		Horse Chestnut	"	"
O	213	16'03		Oak	Near old bowling green	"
O	382	16'05		Sweet Chestnut	Near A370	"
O	384	16'04		Sweet Chestnut	"	"
O	386	15'09		Sweet Chestnut	"	"
O	379	14'00		Oak	"	"
O	380	14'00		Oak	"	"
O	257	U/O		Lime	Old carriageway to bowling green. Quite a few over 10'	"
O	256	U/O		Lime	"	"
O	383	U/O		Oak	Near A370	
O	262	16'02		Beech	Brockley Combe (cut down Spring 2001)	

Brockley Parish   Chelvey Batch

An 18'01 cedar (ref. 121) at Brockley Cottage, cut down Spring 2001. I could see nothing wrong with this magnificent tree and it was one of the largest in North Somerset.

Pri/Open	No.	Size	Feature	Type	Location	Map Ref.
P	133	19'02		Cedar	Brockley fields, South of A370	67/47
P	121	18'01		Cedar	Brockley Cottage (cut down Spring 2001)	"
P	98	17'08		Cypress	Brockley Cottage	"
P	475	15'00		Horse Chestnut	Piggots	"
P	9	14'08		Cedar	Brockley Cottage	"
O	485	14'01		Lime	Off Piggots	"
O	486	M/T		"	"	"
O	487	M/T		"	"	"
O	488	M/T		"	"	"
O	489	M/T		"	"	"
				(regrowing from old stump)		
O	1330	19'06	Pot bellied	Yew	Taps Coombe	"
O	1335	17'00		Oak	"	"
O	1336	16'00		Ash	"	"

❑ ❑ ❑ ❑ ❑

Burrington

There is a 19'00 yew (ref. 462) in Burrington Churchyard. Also a 14'08 pollarded ash (ref. 468) in the woods above Burrington Farm and quite a few ancient hazel coppices.

Langford Court Farm

I noticed a large Oak from the main road and asked Mrs Pearson (the owner) for permission to measure it. Mrs Pearson told me there were other large Oaks on the farm. I found twenty large trees over 14'00. Two Oaks at 20'06 (ref. 145) and 20'02 (ref. 147). This was the old park for Langford House. Private property.

In The Car   Burrington. Across the Mendips to Wells, Priddy or Cheddar.

On Foot   Public Footpaths - Limestone Walk, Churchill Gate, Blackdown, Blagdon, Langford and West Mendip Way (Tynings Farm).

Many thanks to: Mr & Mrs Pearson - The Late Sir John Wills

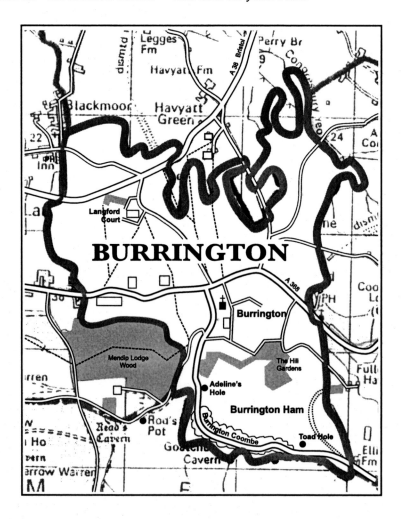

Burrington

Pri/Open	No.	Size	Feature	Type	Location	Map Ref.
O	462	19'01		Yew	Burrington Church Yard	59/47
P	468	14'08	*4 trunks*	Ash	Woods above Burrington Farm	"
O	469	M/T	*Coppice*	Hazel	"	"
O	470	M/T	*Coppice*	Hazel	"	"
P	1442	20'00		Plane	Field, Langford Lane	60/47
P	1443	15'07		Plane	"	"
P	1440	16'01		Lime	Hedgerow, Langford Lane	"
P	1441	M/T	*7 trunks*	Lime	"	"
O	1444	G/O	*Cliff face*	Oak	Rickford Rising	59/48
					Bourne House Area	
P	1552	N/A		Lime	Field	"
P	1553	N/A		Lime	"	"
P	1554	N/A		Lime	"	"
P	1555	N/A		Sweet Chestnut	Garden	
P	1556	N/A		Beech	"	"
P	1557	N/A		Yew	"	"
P	1558	N/A	Creeping M/T	Cypress	"	"
P	1626	W/O		Alder	Rickford stream to Wrington Boundary	"
P	1627	W/O		Alder	"	"
P	1628	W/O		Alder	"	"
					River Yeo, Blagdon Parish to Wrington Parish Border	
P	1629	W/O		Alder		60/47/48/49
P	1630	W/O		Alder	"	"
P	1631	W/O		Alder	"	"
P	1632	W/O		Alder	"	"
P	1633	W/O		Alder	"	"
P	1634	W/O		Alder	"	"
P	1635	W/O		Alder	"	"
P	1636	W/O		Alder	"	"
P	1637	W/O		Alder	"	"
P	1638	W/O		Alder	"	"
P	1639	W/O		Alder	"	"
P	1640	W/O		Alder	"	"
P	1641	W/O		Alder	"	"
P	1642	W/O		Alder	"	"
P	1643	W/O		Alder	"	"
P	1644	W/O		Alder	"	"
P	1645	W/O		Alder	"	"
P	1646	W/O		Alder	"	"
P	1647	W/O		Alder	"	"
P	1648	W/O		Alder	"	"
P	1649	W/O		Ash	"	"
P	1650	W/O		Ash	"	"
P	1651	W/O		Oak	"	"
P	1652	W/O		Oak	"	"

Burrington

Pri/Open	No.	Size	Feature	Type	Location	Map Ref.
O	58	15'08		Wellingtonia	Barley Wood	59/45.46.47
O	16	14'00		Beech	Top of Barley Wood	"
O	134	19'05		Beech	Right of way to encampment, *Beech Avenue*	"
O	123	18'01		Beech	"	"
O	102	17'01		Beech	"	"
O	79	16'01		Beech	"	"
O	80	16'00		Beech	"	"
O	81	16'10		Beech	"	"
O	2105	- - - -		Ash	Rickford to Burrington footpath	59/48

Burrington   Langford Court Farm
(former park land for Langford House)

Note: **Private ground.**   Permission must be sought from Mr & Mrs Pearson (Tel. No. 852638) regarding access

Pri/Open	No.	Size	Feature	Type	Location	Map Ref.
P	145	20'06		Oak	Next to brook	59/60/47
P	147	20'02		Oak	"	"
P	127	18'02		Oak	"	"
P	128	18'09		Oak	"	"
P	577	17'10		Oak	"	"
P	88	16'07		Oak	Field next to road	"
P	90	16'08		Oak	"	"
P	66	15'10		Oak	"	"
P	64	15'11		Oak	"	"
P	65	15'11		Oak	"	"
P	62	15'00		Lime	"	"
P	67	15'05	*Regrowing from stump*	Lime	"	"
P	20	14'07		Oak	"	"
P	27	14'03		Oak	"	"
P	26	14'02		Oak	"	"
P	22	14'09		Maple Plane	"	"
P	25	14'09		Lime	"	"
P	23	14'08		Maple Plane	"	"
P	24	14'06	*Holly growing inside*	Maple Plane	"	"
P	21	14'00		Maple Plane	"	"

Millfort House, Langford

Pri/Open	No.	Size	Feature	Type	Location	Map Ref.
P	2091	20'02		Wellingtonia		59/60/47
P	2092	16'06		Wellingtonia	"	"
P	2093	23'00		Cypress	"	"

The Largest Cypress in North Somerset

Butcombe

Very large Beech
next to Rectory Cottage,
16'05 (ref. 87)

In The Car

Nempnett Thrubwell

Chew Stoke

West Harptree

and onto the

Mendips

On Foot

Two Rivers Way,

Blagdon Lane and
Nempnett Thrubwell

Butcombe Mill Woods
to Blagdon Lake

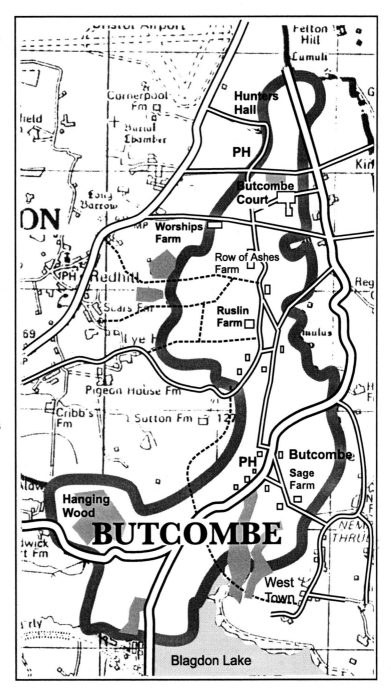

Butcombe

Pri/Open	No.	Size	Feature	Type	Location	Map Ref.
O	87	16'05		Beech	Field next to Rectory Cottage	61/51
O	1436	16'07 *'Home Sweet Home' & M Willmott 1979 carved on trunk*		Beech	Public footpath, Mill Stream Wood to Blagdon Lake	"
O	1509	W/O		Beech	"	"
P	1503	14'09		Beech	Butcombe Court woods	63/51
P	1504	16'09		Horse Chestnut	"	"
P	1505	16'00	*Single trunk, 100' plus tall*	Willow	"	"
P	1506	16'10	*Huge trunk*	Lime	"	"
P	1507	U/O	*Hairy*	Lime	"	"
P	1508	16'02		Beech	Butcombe Court House	"
P	1704	16'08	M/T	Ash	Wood south of Worships Farm	63/50
P	1705	M/T		Ash	"	"
P	2087	22'04		Oak	Above Barley Brook House	61/51
P	2088	22'00	)	Layered	"	"
P	2089	22'00	)	Field Maples	"	"

Wellingtonia and friends at Skinners Lane, Churchill. Ref: 57

Churchill

Extremely large wellingtonia 20'05 (ref. 141) at Skinners Lane.

Also an ancient yew in the Churchyard 16'02 (ref. 265). A copper beech 14'03 (ref. 984) at Baytree House, Dinghurst Road. A spreading oak 16'02 (ref. 819) at Churchill Green Farm.

Many thanks to Mrs Z Day.

Langford

30'01 (ref. 162) Wellingtonia in a field at Springhead Farm. This is one of the largest trees in North Somerset. Private property.

Also two Wellingtonias in the grounds of Jubilee Homes, 227 (ref. 153) and 20'06 (ref. 142).

Private property.

"Take the children/grand-children Bull-Heading in Langford Brook, next to the bridge on the A368, Upper Langford.

Huge spreading Oak on Congresbury Road in a field next to Stoneycroft on the public footpath, 20'01 (ref. 253).

Langford House	Eight trees over 14'00. Plenty over 10'00. Private ground.
Langford	This is the place to find large trees. 29'07 Lime (ref. 541)at base.
Mendip Woods	This tree is over 40'00 measured at 6'00 up and I could probably
(Wildlife Trust Area)	park my truck in it. Another at 25'04 (ref. 542). Thomas' Lime is 22'06 (ref. 552). Thomas helped me to measure this tree. There is

a Beech, 21'07 (ref. 547) which is one of the largest in North Somerset. This wood is also covered in ancient Yews of which only one, that I could find, was over 14'00. It was 14'06 (ref. 561) and growing out of the wall.

In The Car	Churchill - Langford - Wrington - Redhill - Lyehole Butcombe - Blagdon - Charterhouse - Shipham - Churchill
On Foot	Windmill Hill - Limestone Link - Sandford Hill - Dolberrow

Churchill

Pri/Open	No.	Size	Feature	Type	Location	Map Ref.
O	141	20'05		Wellingtonia	Skinners Lane	59/44
O	57	15'01		Wellingtonia	"	"
O	265	16'02		Yew	Churchill Church Yard	60/43
P	266	14'11		Oak	Ivy Lodge, Front Street	59/44
O	726	14'00		Lime	Hillside below quarry	"
O	727	14'02		Lime	"	"
O	816	14'02	*Base measure 3 trunks*	Ash	Windmill Hill	60/44
O	817	M/T	*Split trunk*	Ash	"	"
O	818	16'00	*Wire fence*	Lime	"	"
P	819	16'02	*Split trunk*	Oak	Field, Churhchill Green Farm	60/43
P	820	U/O		Oak	Orchard, Churchill Green	"
P	821	M/T		Sycamore	Churchill pond	"
P	822	M/T	*3 trunks*	Ash	"	"
P	823	15'04		Oak	Field next to Church	"
P	264	14'10		Oak	Church pond street	"
P	984	14'03	*Grafted*	Copper Beech	Baytree House, Dinghurst Road	59/44
P	985	15'01		Wellingtonia	"	"
P	987	14'03		Maple	Field, Baytree House, Dinghurst Rd	"
P	1468	14'03		Lime	Field below Knowle Wood	"
P	1469)	22'07		Lime	Both together, both single trunk and stumpy	"
P	1470)	20'07		Lime		
O	576	M/T	*Coppice*	Hazel	Dolberrow	"
P	1596	N/A		Oak	Orway Porcy House, Stock Lane	61/41
P	1597	N/A		Oak	"	"
O	1668	W/O		Alder	River Yeo	62/46
O	1669	W/O		Alder	River Yeo	"
O	1670	W/O		Alder	"	"
O	1671	W/O		Willow	River Yeo, near Langford Brook	"

Churchill Parish   Langford

Pri/Open	No.	Size	Feature	Type	Location	Map Ref.
P	162	30'01		Wellingtonia	Spring Head Farm. *(Can be seen from A368 - no public access)*	59/46
P	83	16'10		Ash	"	"
P	153	22'07		Wellingtonia	Jubilee House, Langford Road	60/46
P	142	20'06		Wellingtonia	"	"
P	124	1 8'04		Wellingtonia	Redstones, Langford Road	
O	253	20'01		Oak	Field next to Stonycroft, Congresbury Road	62/45
O	252	14'07		Oak	"	"
O	251	14'01		Oak	Lane to Stonycroft	"
P	2104	M/T		Acacia	Acacia Hse, Blackmoor	61/46

Churchill Parish — Langford House

Pri/Open	No.	Size	Feature	Type	Location	Map Ref.
P	235	18'06		Wellingtonia	Langford House	60.61/45.46
P	101	17'00		Cedar	"	"
P	77	16'07		Wellingtonia	"	"
P	55	15'09		Wellingtonia	"	"
P	14	14'10		Oak	"	"
P	15	14'00		Beech	"	"
P	35	M/T		Cypress	"	"
P	36	M/T		Sycamore	"	"
P	1592	15'03		Oak	Field, north boundary	"
P	1593	W/O		Willow	Ditch, north boundary	"
P	1594	W/O		Willow	"	"
P	1595	W/O		Willow	"	"

Churchill Parish Langford — Mendip Woods

Pri/Open	No.	Size	Feature	Type	Location	Map Ref.
O	141	20'05		Wellingtonia	Skinners Lane	59/44
O	82	16'09		Horse Chestnut	FP, Barley Wood	59/45.46.47
O	558	16'00		Lime	Above Spring Head Farm	"
O	559	15'03		Sycamore	"	"
O	546	14'00		Lime	"	"
O	549	14'02		Lime	"	"
O	557	18'04		Lime	"	"
O	562	14'04		Ash	"	"
O	37-46	M/T		Limes	Barley Wood	"
O	550, 551) 553, 554) & 555)	M/T		Limes		"
O	541	29'07		Lime	Wildlife Trust ground	"
O	542	25'04		Lime	Wildlife Trust ground, public footpath	"
O	547	21'07		Beech	Near Wildlife Trust ground	"
P	552	22'06	4 trunks	Lime (Thomas's)	Warren House	"
O	544	19'00		Lime	Near Wildlife Trust ground	"
O	556	16'02		Lime	"	"
O	543	20'11		Oak	Growing out of encampment wall	"
O	545	17'08		Lime	Next to Yew, growing out of encapment wall	59/45. .46.47
O	548	17'08		Lime	Next to wall, encampment	"
O	560	14'04		Lime	Clearing, Barley Wood	"
O	561	14'06		Yew	Clearing, on wall, Barley Wood	"

'Wellingtonia, Ref. 57, 15'01 is now a sculpture at Churchill traffic lights'

"Take the children and grandchildren up to Dolebury Hill Fort and imagine what it was like over 1,000 years ago. Here was the Bristol of this area at that time."

Clapton in Gordano

One 17'07 single trunk Ash (ref. 982) at Gordano Scout Camp.

Nicholas Wood (Private property)

Nine Ash trees all growing from ancient stools. Two over 20'00. Also two pollarded sycamores in the field next to the Church, 27'03 (ref. 705) and 21'02 (ref. 706).

In The Car   See Clevedon

On Foot   Cadbury Camp
Priors Wood, Portbury
Weston Big Wood

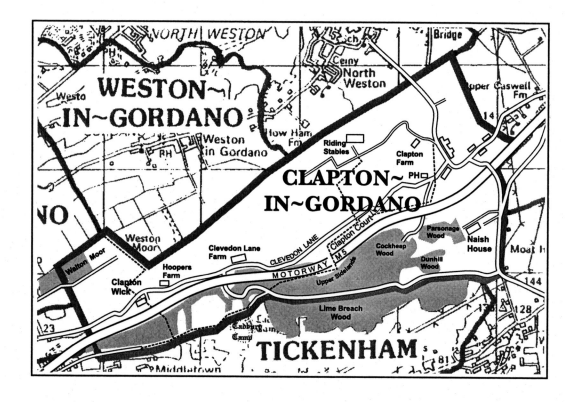

Clapton In Gordano

Pri/Open	No.	Size	Feature	Type	Location	Map Ref.
P	705	27'03	*3 trunks*	Sycamore	Field next to Church (no public access)	72/47
P	706	21'02	*4 trunks*	Sycamore	"	"
P	707	20'02	*3 trunks*	Ash	Nicholas Wood	"
P	708	19'04	*8 trunks*	"	") All	"
P	709	16'02	*5 trunks*	"	") growing	"
P	710	M/T		"	") from	"
P	711	M/T		"	") ancient	"
P	712	15'04	*4 trunks*	"	") stools	"
P	713	20'02	*6 trunks*	"	")	"
P	714	16'08	*5 trunks*	"	")	"
P	715	16'01	*5 trunks*	"	")	"
P	1820	14'02		Beech	Naish House	"
P	1821	16'08		Beech	"	"
P	1822	16'05	*Grafted?*	Beech	"	"
P	1985	20'02	*Stool*	Lime	Wood above Clevedon Lane	73/45
P	1986	M/T	*Stool*	Lime	Lane Farm below M5 Motorway	"
P	1987	M/T	*Stool*	Lime	"	"
P	1988	M/T	*Stool*	Lime	"	"
P	1989	M/T	*Stool*	Lime	"	"
P	1981	17'00	*5 trunk*	Lime	Gordano Scout Camp	73/47
P	1982	17'07	*Single trunk*	Ash	*(Huge spreadingtree)*	"
P	1983	21'07	*5 trunk stool*	Ash	Cookham Wood Lane	"
P	1984	14'10	*80' + tall*	Oak	"	"
O	1972	14'00		Oak	Above M5 viaduct, wood, Clapton Lane Farm	72/45

* Dunhill Wood - Nothing over 14'00

** Parsonage Wood - Nothing over 14'00

Cleeve

Georgian House	Wellingtonia 26'02 (ref. 164) and a 17'01 cedar (ref. 115) which has been hit by lightning. Private property.
Cleeve Court	Private property.
Twin Cedars	This was Cleeve House but was burnt down in 1960. 17'10 cedar (ref. 767) in grounds. Private property.
Brockley Woods	26'06 Oak (ref. 254) just inside the parish boundary. This oak is the largest in North Somerset outside Ashton Court. Many thanks to Geoff Hobbs
In The Car	Cleeve - Wrington - Aldwick - Blagdon - Butcombe - Nempnett Thrubwell - Redhill - Wrington - Cleeve
On Foot	Kings Wood - Wrington Warren - Goblin Combe Claverham Green Pool - Chelvey Church - Brockley Wood

Cleeve   Kings Wood

Pri/Open	No.	Size	Feature	Type	Location	Map Ref.
P	1317	15'09		Yew	Above Dave Ridleys farm	64.65/44.45.46
P	1318	14'07		Yew	") Many	"
P	1319	M/T	*Old Stools*	Lime	") ancient	"
P	1320	M/T		Lime	") Limes,	"
P	1321	M/T		Lime	") Ash	"
P	1322	M/T		Lime	") and	"
P	1323	M/T		Lime	") Yew	"
P	1324	15'03	*Growing out of cliff*	Yew	Valley track right of Dave Ridleys farm	"
P	132S	14'03	*One trunk cut*	Yew	"	"
P	1326	14'03	*M/T*	Lime	"	"
P	1327	M/T		Yew	"	"
P	1328	16'00		Yew	"	"
P	1329	14'04	*Split*	Oak	"	"
P	1343	M/T	*Old stool*	Lime	East of Bickley House	"
P	1344	M/T	*"*	Lime	"	"
P	1345	M/T	*"*	Lime	"	"
P	1346	M/T	*"*	Lime	"	"
P	1347	M/T	*"*	Lime	"	"
P	1348	M/T	*"*	Lime	Next to footpath above small quarry	"
P	1349	M/T	*"*	Lime	"	"
P	1350	17'05	*9 trunk,*	Ash	Above small quarry	"
						base measure
P	1351	M/T	*8 trunk*	Ash	East of Bickley House	"
P	13S2	M/T	*8 trunk*	Ash	"	"
P	1353	M/T	*4 trunk*	Ash	"	"

Many thanks to Mr & Mrs Dave Ridley

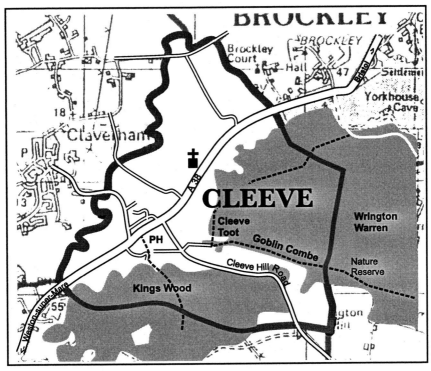

"Goblin Coombe Nature Reserve — well worth a visit."

Cleeve

Pri/Open	No.	Size	Feature	Type	Location	Map Ref.
P	164	26'02		Wellingtonia	Georgian House *(no public access)*	65/46
P	115	17'01	*Hit by lightning*	Cedar	"	"
P	152	21'05		Cypress	Cleeve Court *(no public access)*	"
P	32	14'10		Wellingtonia	"	"
P	33	14'08		Horse Chestnut	"	"
O	70	15'06		Beech	Goblin Coombe	"
P	767	17'10		Cedar	Twin Cedars (was Cleeve House burned down in the 60's?)	66/45
O	1196	17'05	Pollard	Oak	West field, Littlewood Lane	"
O	1197	M/T	*Double rooted*	Willow	Pond, north of Cleeve House Farm	"
O				Hornbeam	West field, Littlewood Lane	"
O	1314	U/O		Lime	Cleeve Hill Road	65/46
P	1312	14'08	M/T	Sweet Chestnut	Stones Wood	"
P	1311	19'04	M/T	Sweet Chestnut	"	"
O	1315	15'08	*6 trunks*	Beech	PFP off Cleeve Hill Road near Stones Wood	"
						"
O	1316	M/T	*9 trunks*	Lime	"	"
P	254	26'06		Oak	Brokley Wood (in Cleeve Parish)	64/46
O	2087	14'04		Copper Beech	Westhanger House	65/45

Many thanks to Mr & Mrs Grimley

Clevedon

There is a 22'09 plane (ref. 154) and a 20'04 three trunked sweet chestnut (ref. 184) in the grounds of Clevedon Court.

In a field next to Clevedon Court is a 20'06 oak (ref. 185).

Largest single trunk Holm Oak in North Somerset, 16'02 (ref. 1932). Above and to the right of Clevedon Court. This is not only the largest but also a superb example

In The Car

Clevedon

Portishead Coast Road (good views)

Portbury

Failand

Clapton in Gordano

Clevedon Lane

On Foot

Coastal Walk, Portishead

Castle Hill

Walton in Gordano

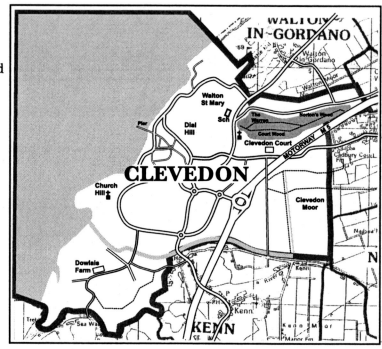

"Take the children crabbing by Clevedon Pier"

Clevedon

Pri/Open	No.	Size	Feature	Type	Location	Map Ref.
O	704	15'11	*M/T*	Oak	St John's Church, St John's Road	71/41
O	1799	14'00	*Split*	Beech	Public foot path, Strawberry Hill	"
O	1954	G/O	*Layered*	Sycamore	Old main road next to motorway bridge	72/42
O	1970	M/T	*7 trunks*	Oak	Ancient bridleway Norton Wood	72/43
P	1971	M/T	*8 trunks*	Ash	Wood above Clevedon Riding Centre, Norton Wood Lane	"
P	185	20'06		Oak	Field off of Clevedon Court	71/42

Clevedon

Clevedon Court

Pri/Open	No.	Size	Feature	Type	Location	Map Ref.
					Clevedon Court	
O	154	22'09		Plane/Maple		72/42
O	184	20'04	3 trunks	Sweet Chestnut		"
					Woods. Clevedon Court Old Estate	
O	1930	17'00	4 trunks	Horse Chestnut	East of House	72/42
O	1931	16'00	3 trunks	Horse Chestnut	Lower drive	"
O	1932	16'02	Single trunk	Holm Oak	Fork in lower path	"
			*largest Holm Oak in North Somerset			
O	1933	22'00	Decayed trunk		Lime Lower path	"
O	1934	M/T		Lime	"	"
O	193S	M/T		Lime	"	"
O	1936	M/T		Lime	"	"
O	1937	M/T		Lime	"	"
O	1938	M/T		Lime	"	"
O	1939	M/T		Holm Oak	"	"
O	1940	M/T		Holm Oak	"	"
O	1941	M/T		Holm Oak	Lime Lower path	72/42
O	1942	14'00	Single trunk	Sycamore	"	"
O	1943	G/O	Collapsed across path	Holm Oak	Above Clevedon Court	"
O	1944	17'00		Pine	West of old quarry	"
O	1946	G/O	Collapsed	Pine	Near path, folly	"
O	1947	22'00	Hairy	Lime	"	"
O	1948	U/O	Hairy	Lime	"	"
O	1949	U/O	Hairy	Lime	"	"
O	19S0	U/O	Hairy	Lime	"	"
O	1951	U/O	Hairy	Lime	"	"
O	1952	14'06		Holm Oak	Next to motorway fence	72/42
O	1953	G/O	Bulbous trunk	Lime	Lower path towards motorway	"
					Clevedon Court Old Estate	
O	1961	14'06	3 trunks	Beech	Swiss valley wood	74/42
O	1962	17'06	4 trunks	Oak	"	"
O	1963	M/T	5 trunks, initials AC, SC, JC	Beech	"	"
O	1964	17'04	3 trunks	Beech	" (near quarry)	"
O	1965	14'00	Split	Sycamore	"	"
O	1966	M/T		Holm Oak	Court Hill	"
O	1967	U/O	Hairy	Lime	"	"
O	1967	14'00	80 + tall	Horse Chestnut	"	"
O	1969	15'05	Split	Holm Oak	"	"

Many thanks to Mrs W Knight

Congresbury

A large spreading Lucombe oak 18'07 (ref. 131) at Rhodyate Lodge. This tree is not pollarded and is huge. Private property.

25'00 single trunk Oak at Mendip Green Golf Course (ref. 258) which is second largest Oak outside of Ashton Court.

In The Car

Congresbury -- Wrington - Aldwick

Blagdon - Charterhouse - Shipham

Churchill - Langford

Congresbury

On Foot

Congresbury Church and the Millenium Bridge are both worth a look with good food at the Ship and Castle.

Public Footpaths:

Two Rivers Way

Kingswood

"Feed the ducks from the beautifully designed Millennium Bridge at Congresbury"

Many thanks to Henry Collins

Oak - 25'00   Ref: 258
The Author seen supporting this aged oak at Mendip Spring Golf Club, Congresbury

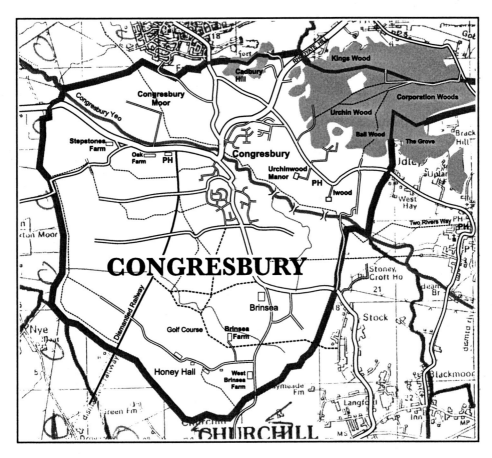

Congresbury

Pri/Open	No.	Size	Feature	Type	Location	Map Ref.
P	258	25'00	"	Oak	Mendip Green Golf Course (no public access)	61/44
P	263	18'00	"	Oak	"	"
P	131	18'07	*Spreading*	Luncombe Oak	Rhodyate Lodge Field	64/44
P	69	15'08	*Pollard*	Ash	"	"
P	30	14'04	"	Oak	"	"
P	31	14'01	"	Oak	"	"
P	212	16'11	"	Oak	Woodlands Field	"
P	825	14'04	8 trunks	Holm Turkey Oak	Woodlands Wood	"
P	207	18'06		Oak	Field next to Woodlands (Parish Boundary)	"
P	231	14'09		Beech	Field edge next to Woodlands	"
P	1994	14'07		Willow	Brook near Well Farm	"

Congresbury

Pri/Open	No.	Size	Feature	Type	Location	Map Ref.
O	29	14'03		Beech	Churchyard	63/43
O	48	F/O		Oak	Next to Millenimum Bridge	"
O	47	W/O		Oak	Millenium Field	"
O	824	14'06	*Pollard*	Oak	Field next to river, Iwood Farm	63/45
P	1667	N/A	*Spreading*	Oak	Inwood Manor Tennis Court	"
O	230	15'06		Willow	River Yeo, Inwood Lane	"
P	261	14'01	*Lopped*	Horse Chesnut	West Barn, Westhay Road	"
P	1286	M/T	*Old stool*	Lime	Ball Urchin Wood	64/45.46
P	1287	M/T	"	Lime	"	"
P	1288	M/T	"	Lime	"	"
P	1289	M/T	"	Lime	"	"
P	1290	M/T	"	Lime	"	"
P	1291	M/T	"	Lime	"	"
P	1292	M/T	"	Lime	"	"
P	1293	M/T	"	Lime	"	"
P	1294	M/T	"	Lime	"	"
P	1295	M/T	"	Lime	"	"
P	1296	14'02	*5 trunks, pollard*	Ash	"	"
P	1297	14'05	*4 trunks*	Ash	"	"
P	1298	M/T	*7 trunks*	Ash	"	"
P	1299	18'10	*9 trunks*	Lime	"	"
P	1300	15'05	*4 trunks*	Lime	"	"
P	1301	15'07	*6 trunks*	Lime	"	"
P	1302	15'00	*) Growing on*	Yew	" "	
P	1303	14'02	*)top of a rock*	Yew		
O	1304	18'08		Lime	Near Woolmers Wood, South above Woolmers	64/45
O	1305	14'04		Lime	"	"
O	1306	M/T		Lime	"	"
O	1307	M/T		Lime	"	"
O	1308	M/T		Lime	"	"
O	1309	M/T		Lime	"	"
O	1310	M/T		Lime	"	"

Easton in Gordano

Very large 23'03 wellingtonia (ref. 494) in the Church grounds. 16 trees over 14'00 at Markham Brook. 23'00 extremely large oak, not pollarded , (ref. 868) at Ferndale, Markham Brook and 21'05 five trunk lime (ref. 867). Private property.

Ham Green House

Five cedars over 14'00. 22'00 hollow, burnt ancient Oak (ref. 503) near Ham Green House Orchard, near public footpath.

Ham Green Playing Fields

Two lime trees 14'08 (ref. 497) and 14'00 (ref. 498). Huge magnificent trees with lots of ingrowing in upper branches.

Riverbank Woods

19'08 unpollarded oak next to the Lookout. Keep children and dogs away as the banks of the river are very steep.

Developers at Ham Green have done a superb job of looking after the existing trees and planting new ones.

In The Car

Easton in Gordano Long Ashton
Barrow Gurney
Winford
Chew Magna
Dundry
(views across Bristol)
Cambridge Batch
Failand
Easton in Gordano

On Foot

Unusual footpath accross River Avon next to motorway

Leigh Woods

Riverside Way Walk

Charlton Farm via Hails Wood

Markham Brook

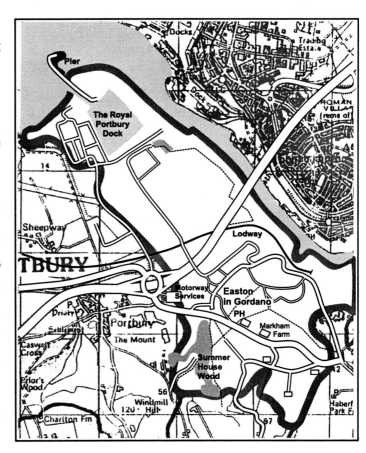

Easton in Gordano

Pri/Open	No.	Size	Feature	Type	Location	Map Ref.
O	494	23'03		Wellingtonia	Church Grounds	75/51
O	509	14'01	*Long narrow trunk*	Lime	Marsh Lane	"
O	490	M/T	*Layered*	Sycamore	Church Wall	"
O	491	M/T		Sycamore	"	"
O	492	M/T		Sycamore	"	"
O	493	M/T		Sycamore	"	"
P	853	16'08	*8 trunks*	Lime	Markham Brook	74/53
P	854	18'07	*6 trunks*	Lime	"	"
P	855	M/T	*3 trunks*	Lime	"	"
P	856	M/T	*3 trunks*	Lime	"	"
P	857	M/T	*5 trunks*	Lime	"	"
P	858	M/T	*3 trunks1*	Lime	"	"
P	859	M/T	*5 trunks*	Oak	"	"
P	860	16'04	M/T	Lime	"	"
P	861	16'02		Ash	"	"
P	862	M/T	*3 trunk*	Ash	"	"
P	863	15'08		Ash	"	"
P	864	14'01		Ash	"	"
P	865	14'05	*4 trunks*	Ash	"	"
P	866	M/T	*5 trunks*	Field Maple	"	"
P	867	21'05	*5 trunks*	Lime	Ferndale, Markham Brook	
P	868	23'00	*Very large, not pollarded*	Oak	"	"
P	1131	15'01		Beech	Hailswood	74/51

** *No small children due to open hidden quarry cliffs* **

Pri/Open	No.	Size	Feature	Type	Location	Map Ref.
P	1132	M/T	*7 trunks*	Ash	Hailswood	
P	1133	M/T	*5 trunks*	Ash	"	"
P	1134	M/T	*3 trunks*	Ash	"	"
P	1241	18'07	*7 trunks*	Ash	"	"
P	1242	18'03	*5 trunks*	Ash	"	"
P	1243	15'00	*4 trunks*	Ash	"	"
P	1244	16'07	*3 trunks, stool*	Lime	"	"
P	124S	19'06	*80' tall*	Lime	"	"
O	1246	16'08	*Pollard*	Oak	Field, public foot path south of Hails Wood	"
O	1247	MIT	*Stool*	Alder	Hails Wood Brook, public foot path	"
O	1248	14'10	*11 trunks at 5'00*	Alder	"	"
O	1249	MIT	*Stool*	Alder	Hails Wood Brook, public footpath	"
O	1250	15'00	*Twin trunks*	Alder	"	"
P	1251	17'00	*3 trunks*	Alder	" *(private)*	"
P	1252	F/O	*20'00 + at 8'00, pollard*	Oak	Field, south of Coombe Lane	74/51
P	1135	16'05	*Not pollard, Huge*	Oak	Field, south of Hailswood	"

"Take the children and grand-children safely on their bikes under the Suspension Bridge on the River Avon cycleway"

Easton in Gordano   Ham Green

Pri/Open	No.	Size	Feature	Type	Location	Map Ref.
O	503	22'00	*Hollow, burn't*	Oak	Near orchard, Ham Green House	75/53
P	500	18'01		Cedar	Lawn, Ham Green House	"
P	S06	18'10		Cedar	"	"
P	505	15'09		Wellingtonia	"	"
P	499	14'02		Cedar	"	"
P	501	14'01		Beech	"	"
P	502	15'01		Oak	Near orchard, Ham Green House	"
P	S04	17'09		Cedar	Lawn, Ham Green House	"
P	508	N/A		Cedar	Stables, Ham Green House	"
O	496	16'05	*Cut down 2001*	Sweet Chestnut	Ham Green playing fields	"
O	495	15'07	*Lopped*	Sweet Chestnut	"	"
O	497	14'08		Lime	"	"
O	498	14'00		Lime	"	"
P	826	14'08		Oak	Riverbank woods, Ham Green House	"
P	827	14'01	*Vertical*	Ash	"	"
P	828	M/T	*Split trunk*	Lime	"	"
P	829	M/T		Lime	"	"
P	830	M/T		Lime	"	"
P	831	M/T		Lime	"	"
P	832	15'05		Horse Chestnut	"	"
P	833	16'00	*Huge branch*	Oak	"	"
P	834	19'08		Oak	Next to lookout, riverbank woods Ham Green House	"

'Hairy Trees' - Ref. 497, 498

Flaxbourton

Wellingtonia 24'01 (ref. 240) at Eastfield House. Four ancient yews at The Grange (multi-trunks). Oak (ref. 739). Where is has been pollarded it is over 25'00. This tree is huge and is in the field West of the old hospital. It has ropes for children to swing on.

There was an extremely large 40'00 plus Oak in Ten Acres Field which was destroyed by fire in 1955. This could have easily been the largest tree in North Somerset.

Many thanks to Maurice Atherton for this information.

In The Car	Flax Bourton - Backwell Hill Road - Lulsgate - Winford Manor Regil - Chew Stoke - Chew Magna - Dundry - Barrow Gurney Flax Bourton
On Foot	Wraxall Sidelands Wood - Jubilee Stone - Barrow Gurney

Flaxbourton

Pri/Open	No.	Size	Feature	Type	Location	Map Ref.
P	240	24'01	S/T	Wellingtonia	Eastfield House *(no public access)*	69/51
O	378	24'08	M/T	Yew	The Grange *(no public access)*	"
O	244	17'04	*3 trunks*	Sycamore	Opposite Court House	"
P	241	16'05		Oak	Field next to Eastfield House	"
P	375	16'08	M/T	Yew	The Grange	"
P	376	14'01	M/T	Yew	"	"
P	377	14'07	M/T	Yew	"	"
O	536	19'00		Oak	Parish boundary, track below A371	69/50
O	734	17'02	*Pollard*	Crack Willow	Bathing Pond Brook	70/50
O	735	14'01	Pollard	Crack Willow	"	"
O	736	U/O	Pollard	Crack Willow	"	"
O	737	18'06		Oak	Field West of old hospital	69/51
O	738	16'00		Oak	"	"
O	739	16'03	*25' at pollard*	Oak	"	"
O	740	U/O		Oak	"	"
O	741	16'02	*In ditch*	Oak	"	"
O	742	14'00	*Pollard*	Ash	Field West of old hospital	"
		(growing from very old pollard)				"
O	743	15'06		Oak	"	"
P	1041	14'10	*Gate*	Oak	Hedgerow, North Breech Hill Wood	"
P	1042	14'00		Oak	Breech Hill Wood East	"
P	1043	M/T	*18' plus trunk*	Oak	"	"
P	1044	M/T	*Coppice*	Oak	Hedgerow Breech Hill Wood East	"
P	1045	M/T	*Coppice*	Oak	"	"
P	1046	14'03		Oak	"	"
P	1047	15'07		Oak	"	"
P	1048	14'01	*Coppice*	Oak	Parkland North (left) of Barrow Court	68/51

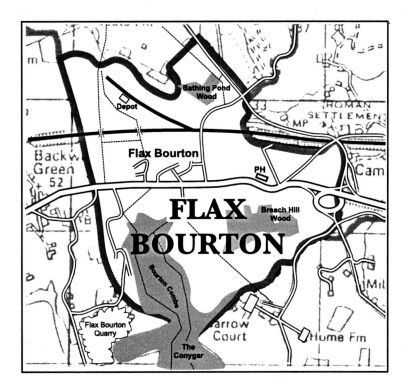

Flaxbourton

Pri/Open	No.	Size	Feature	Type	Location	Map Ref.
P	1404	14'08		Oak	Parkland North (rt) of Barrow Court	68/51
P	1405	14'08		Oak	"	"
O	1370	M/T		Sycamore	Bourton Combe Woods, left side	68/50
O	1371	M/T		Sycamore	"	"
O	1372	M/T		Sycamore	"	"
O	1373	M/T		Sycamore	"	"
O	1374	M/T		Sycamore	"	"
O	1375	M/T		Sycamore	"	"
O	1376	M/T		Sycamore	"	"
O	1377	M/T		Sycamore	"	"
O	1378	M/T		Sycamore	"	"
O	1379	M/T		Sycamore	Bourton Combe Woods, left side	68/50
O	1380	M/T		Beech	"	"
O	1281	M/T		Beech	"	"
O	1382	M/T		Beech	"	"
O	1383	15'00	*7 trunk stool*	Lime	Bourton Combe Woods, right side	"
O	1384	17'02	*6 trunk*	Lime	Bourton Combe Woods, lower	"
O	138S	M/T	*6 trunk*	Lime	"	"
O	1386	M/T	*6trunk*	Lime	"	"
O	1387	M/T	*6trunk*	Lime	"	"
O	1388	14'10		Oak	"	"
O	1389	16'11	*Old marking*	Beech	Bourton Combe Woods, r/h side	"

Flaxbourton

Pri/Open	No.	Size	Feature	Type	Location	Map Ref.
O	1390	M/T		Sycamore	Bourton Combe Woods, middle below quarry	68/50
O	1391	M/T		Sycamore	"	"
O	1392	M/T	*This area is*	"	"	"
O	1393	M/T	*covered in*	"	"	"
O	1394	M/T	*Rhodedendrums*	"	"	"
O	1395	M/T		Yew	"	"
O	1396	M/T		Yew	"	"
O	1406	16'10	*60' + tall*	Oak	Bourton Combe, Footpath leading to disused quarry	"
O	1407	M/T		Sycamore	"	"
P	1408	U/O	*One of 3*	Lime	Field near pond, right of Bourton Combe Wood	"
P	1409	20'00	*25' + at 10' huge*	Oak	"	"
P	1410	14'00	*Collapsed across stream*	Oak	Spring/brook, North of Barrow Court	"
P	1411	14'11		Oak	"	"
P	1412	16'04	*20' + root base, decayed, hollow*	Ash	Near spring/brook, North of Barrow Court	"

Maurice Atherton seen with 40' Oak in Ten Acre Field, subsequently destroyed by fire in 1955

Hutton

Benthill Woods

Eighteen trees over 14'00 of which twelve are ash growing out of ancient stools. One is 20'07 (ref. 757) with seven trunks.

In The Car   See Banwell
Outstanding views across Somerset Levels along Roman Road

On Foot   West Mendip Way - Banwell Hill - Christon

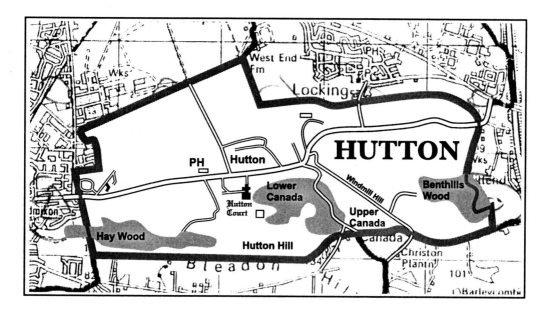

Hutton

Pri/Open	No.	Size	Feature	Type	Location	Map Ref.
					Hutton Hill Woods	
P	1488	M/T	*Split*	Ash	Middle	58/35
P	1489	M/T	*8 trunk stool*	Ash	Small tree, top near metal hut	"
P	1490	M/T	*4 trunk stool*	Ash	Top left	"
P	1491	M/T	*Triple stool*	Lime	Bottom left	"
P	1492	15'00	*Single trunk*	Lime	Bottom left	"
P	1493	U/O		Ash	Hay Woods above Manor Farm	58/34
P	1494	U/O		Ash	"	"
P	1495	14'00	*Hollow*	Ash	"	"

Many thanks to Eddie Langford of Oldmixon

Hutton

Pri/Open	No.	Size	Feature	Type	Location	Map Ref.
P	744	1 6'08	4 trunks	Ash	Benthills Woods *(All Ashes multi trunk and pollards)*	58/37
P	745	M/T	*7 trunks*	Ash	Benthills Woods	"
P	746	14'05	*7 trunks*	Ash	"	"
P	747	15'02	*7 trunks*	Ash	"	"
P	748	16'02	*5 trunks*	Ash	"	"
P	749	14'00	*6 trunks*	Ash	"	"
P	750	M/T	*Coppice*	Hazel	"	"
P	7S1	16'09	*3 trunks*	Ash	"	"
P	752	15'07	*Split trunk*	Oak	"	"
P	753	14'08	*4 trunks*	Oak	"	"
P	754	15'09	*5 trunks*	Ash	"	"
P	755	15'06	*4 trunks 1 snapped*	Ash	"	"
P	756	16'04	*4 trunks*	Ash	"	"
P	757	20'07	*7 trunks 1 snapped*	Ash	"	"
P	758	M/T	*6 trunks*	Ash	"	"
P	7S9	M/T	*5 trunks*	Ash	"	"
P	760	16'05	*5 trunks*	Ash	"	"
P	761	15'02	*6 trunks*	Ash	"	"
P	762	M/T	*Coppice*	Hazel	Next to wall above Benthills Woods	"
O	797	M/T	*4 trunks coppice*	Ash	On public bridleway, Lower Canada Small Holding	"
O	1472	21'02	*Triple trunk*	Cherry	Public foot path above Elborough Woods	"
P	1473	14'02	*Single trunk*	Ash	Elborough Woods, top left	"
P	1474	21'05	*5 trunks*	Ash	"	"
P	1475	M/T	*Old stool*	Ash	Elborough Woods, top left	58/37
P	1476	M/T	*Old stool*	Ash	Elborough Woods, top left	"
P	1477	M/T	"	Ash	"	"
P	1478	M/T	"	Ash	"	"
P	1479	M/T	"	Ash	"	"
P	1480	M/T	"	Ash	"	"

Many thanks to Mr Curry

Long Ashton

21 '10 dead oak tree at Gatcombe Court. Dead for over 60 years and still standing. Private property. Many thanks to Charles Clark for this information. 14'06 spreading sycamore (ref. 572) at the Iron Plantation. 18'05 cedar (ref. 309) at Glebe Close. 30 plus Wellingtonias over 14'00 at Ashton Hill Planation, the most in North Somerset in one area - well worth a visit. Many thanks to Mr & Mrs Bob Cook for this information.

There is no need to mention Ashton Court trees as they are well recorded already. If you have not visited beore and you like trees then you must go there. I did speak to an old gentleman about the Wellingtonias that Bristol City Council were talking about cutting down, this is what he had to say:

> *"Do people go to Ashton Court because of the house or the trees? If you knocked the house down and kept the trees, people would still flock there. If you cut down the trees and kept the house, nobody would bother."*

If the trees do go there will be a magnificent view of Bedminster Industrial Estate.

Out of the 6 Wellingtonia trees under threat by Bristol City Council, 5 of them are within the 25 largest of any type of tree in North Somerset, out of over 2000 trees. They are also the 2nd, 5th, 6th and 7th largest of this species in North Somerset. If left alone, in the future they could well be the largest trees in the whole of North Somerset as they are extremely fast growing and still babies.

Leigh Woods near the Suspension Bridge - I started to do Leigh Woods towards the end of my survey and was really surprised to find a 29'00 Lime (ref. 1523), a 29'11 Lime (ref. 1524) and a 25'00 Lime (ref. 2075). Also there was the remains of a burnt out Lime which was 30'00 plus. These are all at the tip of Nightingale Valley going towards the Suspension Bridge up in the cliffs.

DO NOT TAKE SMALL CHILDREN AS GROUND IS UNSTABLE.

In The Car   See Flax Bourton

On Foot   Ashton Court

              Monarch Way

              Ashton Hill Plantation
              (30 plus Wellingtonias
              over 14'00)

18'00 Cedar • Ref: 309
Glebe Close, Long Ashton

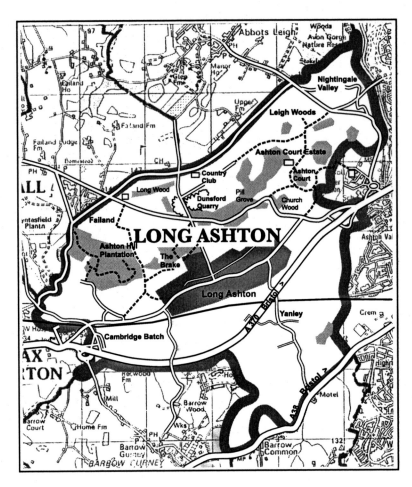

"Take the children to Brunel's Suspension Bridge and on to the Observatory and Caves – tremendous views"

Long Ashton

Pri/Open	No.	Size	Feature	Type	Location	Map Ref.
O	309	18'05		Cedar	Glebe Close	70/54
P	243	21'10	*Pollard*	Oak	Gatcombe Court	"
				(This tree is dead but still standing for over 60 years)		
P	242	14'03	*Pollard*	Oak	Gatcombe Court	"
O	572	14'06	*Spreading*	Sycamore	Iron Plantation	70/53
P	851	14'05		Oak	Cricket Club	70/55
P	852	17'05		Oak	Yanley Farm field	"
O	869	15'10	*Pollard*	Ash	Fenns field	70/53 "
P	870	M/T	*Stool*	Field Maple	Fenns Wood	"
P	871	M/T		Ash	"	"

Long Ashton

Pri/Open	No.	Size	Feature	Type	Location	Map Ref.
O	872	14'00		Lime	The Brake	70/55
O	873	18'07		Lime	"	"
O	874	14'00		Oak	Next to gate, lower entrance to The Brake	"
P	1560	17'05	Base measure 4 trunks	Ash	Cambridge Batch	69/52
P	1561	15'00	Base measure	Sycamore	"	"
P	1788	14'06		Oak	Gatcombe Farm pond	"

Many thanks to   Dick Pearce, Bob Cook and Mr & Mrs Charles Clark

Long Ashton   Leigh Woods

Pri/Open	No.	Size	Feature	Type	Location	Map Ref.
P	2083	15'04		Oak	Burwalls House grounds	72/56
O	2084	14'05	25' at 8'	Oak	Burwalls House woods	""
O	2085	14'06	4 trunks	Horse Chestnut	"	"
O	2086	M/T		Sycamore	"	"
O	466	17'00		Oak	Rownham Hill, near Bristol boundary	"
P	467	15'10		Wellingtonia	Rownham Hill	"
P	1994	16'02	Split	Luncombe Oak	Raynethatch North Road	"
P	1518	N/A		Oak	Lake House, Vicarage Road	"
P	1519	N/A		Oak	Robert Court	"
P	1995	14'02		Sycamore	Rownham House Estate	"
P	1996	15'04		Sycamore	"	"
O	1520	14'09	Dead	Oak	Leigh Woods, Nightingale Valley	73/56
O	1521	14'00		Oak	"	"
O	1522	18'08		Oak	"	"
O	1523	29'01	Stool	Lime	"	"
O	1524	29'11	Stool, split	Lime	"	"
O	1525	D/T	29'+	Lime	"	"
O	1526	15'08	Next to stone wall	Beech	Leigh Woods	"
P	2002	14'06	Pollard	Oak	Gatcombe Hill	"
O	2062	15'01		Oak	Leigh Woods, next to pond	"
O	2063	22'00	Single trunk	Lime	"	"
O	2064	16'00	Fallen	Lime	"	"
O	2078	19'00		Lime	Leigh Woods, below Suspension Bridge	"
O	2079	U/O	Collapsed	Lime	"	"
O	2080	U/O	Collapsed	Lime	"	"
O	2081	U/O	Split	Lime	North slope, Nightingale Valley	"
0	2082	14'10	Single trunk	Lime	"	"

"Take the children and grand-children safely on their bikes under the Suspension Bridge on the River Avon cycleway"

Long Ashton

Ashton Court

Pri/Open	No.	Size	Feature	Type	Location	Map Ref.
					Summerhouse Plantation	
O	347	30'00	*Hollow*	Oak	Top left side	71 & 72/55.56
O	163	28'05	*35' base*	Oak	Bottom right side	"
O	341	22'03		Sycamore	Middle	"
O	92	16'00		Sycamore	?	"
O	343	16'07		Oak	?	"
O	346	16'04		Oak	?	"
O	68	15'04	*Tall*	Sweet Chestnut		"
O	342	15'02		Oak		"
O	345	15'04		Oak		"
O	337	14'00		Horse Chestnut		"
O	338	14'05		Horse Chestnut		"
O	340	14'09		Oak		"
O	344	14'00		Oak		"
					Ashton Court House Area	
O	158	28'01	*Spur*	Wellingtonia	UNDER THREAT	"
O	159	26'01		Wellingtonia	UNDER THREAT	"
O	160	25'11		Wellingtonia	UNDER THREAT	"
O	161	25'07		Wellingtonia	UNDER THREAT	"
O	155	23'10		Wellingtonia	UNDER THREAT	"
O	156	23'04		Wellingtonia	UNDER THREAT	"
O	150	21'06		Beech		"
O	isi	21'02		Sweet Chestnut		"
O	139	20'03		Wellingtonia	Near gate	"
O	140	20'09		Wellingtonia		"
0	132	19'08		Wellingtonia		"
O	96	17'10	*Split*	Cedar		"
O	97	17'10		Wellingtonia		"
					Doomsday Oak Area	
O	326	23'10		Oak	Doomsday Oak	71 & 72/55.56
O	325	24'04		Oak	"	"
O	327	23'06		Sweet Chestnut	Below Doomsday Oak	"
O	331	23'02		"	"	"
O	154	22'09		"	"	"
O	332	22'11		"	"	"
O	335	22'02		"	"	"
O	333	21'01		"	"	"
O	328	20'09		"	"	"
O	329	20'06		"	"	"
O	334	20'05		"	"	"
O	327	17'05		"	"	"
O	322	17'11		"	"	"

Long Ashton   Ashton Court

Pri/Open	No.	Size	Feature	Type	Location	Map Ref.
					Doomsday Oak Area	
O	74	16'06		Sweet Chestnut	Below Doomsday Oak	71 & 72/55.56
O	319	16'01		"	"	"
O	323	16'02		"	"	"
					Church Lodge Area	
O	285	22'06		Oak		"
O	298	21'10		Oak		"
O	281	20'06		Oak		"
O	288	19'04		Oak		"
O	296	18'11		Oak		"
O	297	18'03		Oak		"
O	300	18'06		Oak		"
O	293	17'04		Oak		"
O	294	17'04		Oak		"
O	301	17'02		Oak		"
O	287	16'09		Sweet Chestnut		"
O	291	16'00		Oak		"
O	299	16'00	Dead	Oak		"
O	305	16'09		Oak		"
O	306	16'07		Oak		"
					Wellingtonia Avenue Area	
O	353	22'04		Wellingtonia		"
O	356	17'05		Wellingtonia		"
O	357	16'07		Wellingtonia		"
O	355	15'01		Wellingtonia		"
O	352	14'09		Oak		"
O	351	14'09		Oak		"
O	358	U/O		Lime	Next to wall	"
O	359	U/O		Lime		"
O	360	U/O		Lime		"
					Golf Course Area	
O	137	19'03		Oak		71 & 72/55.56
O	365	18'06		Oak		"
O	366	16'06		Oak		"
O	363	16'00	Single trunk burnt	Ash		"
						"
O	367	15'03		Oak		"
O	362	15'00		Oak		"
O	361	14'03	Split	Oak	Next to wall	"
O	364	14'02		Oak		"
					College Grounds in Bristol City	
O	282	24'09		Wellingtonia		"
					Old Deer Park Area	
O	412	30'03	Hollow	Oak	Woods	"
O	461	29'01	Hollow	Oak	Field	"
O	414	23'00	Hollow	Oak		"

Long Ashton

Ashton Court

Pri/Open	No.	Size	Feature	Type	Location	Map Ref.
					Old Deer Park Area	
O	460	22'02		Oak	Field	71 & 72/55.56
O	415	21'10		Oak		"
O	416	21'04		Oak		"
O	387	20'05	Burnt	Oak	Near gate	"
O	417	20'08		Oak	Above footpath	
O	418	20'08		Oak	Above footpath	"
O	389	19'08		Oak	Below Old Deer Park	
O	419	19'03		Oak	Above footpath	"
O	420	19'03		Oak		"
O	421	19'05		Oak		"
O	459	19'00	Huge, not Pollarded	Oak	Field	"
O	390	18'08		Oak	Below Old Deer Park	"
O	422	18'01		Oak	By top fence	"
O	423	18'07		Oak		"
O	424	18'08		Oak		"
O	454	18;00	Dead	Oak		"
O	457	18'11		Oak	Near lower gate	"
O	425	17'09		Oak	Above footpath	"
O	426	17'03		Oak		"
O	455	1 7'4		Oak	Above footpath	"
O	391	16'11		Oak		"
O	388	15'02		Oak	Below Old Deer Park	"
O	445	14'04		Plane	Lower field	"
O	446	14'09		Lime	Lower field	"
O	447	14'02		Beech	Lower field	"
O	448	14'04		Oak	Below Old Deer Park	"
O	458	14'05		Lime	Field	"
O	427	16'01		Oak	Above footpath	"
O	428	16'08		Oak		"
O	429	16'08		Oak		"
O	430	16'06		Oak		"
O	431	16'S		Oak		"
O	432	16'09		Oak		"
O	433	16'02		Oak		"
O	434	16'10		Oak		"
O	435	16'02		Oak		"
O	436	16'11	Fern l2' up	Oak		"
O	437	16'00		Oak		"
O	438	16'00		Oak		"
O	439	16'08		Oak		"
O	456	16'05	Dead	Oak		"
O	440	15'06		Oak		"

Long Ashton
Ashton Court

Pri/Open	No.	Size	Feature	Type	Location	Map Ref.
					Old Deer Park Area	
O	441	15'08		Oak		71 & 72/55.56
O	442	15'08	Next to Elder	Oak		"
O	443	15'11		Oak		"
O	444	15'00		Oak		"
O	449	14'09		Oak		"
O	450	14'05		Oak		"
O	451	14'09		Oak		"
O	452	14'10		Oak		"
O	453	U/O		Oak		"
O	395	U/O		Oak	Next to fence	"
O	396	U/O		Oak	Top right side of drive	"
O	136	19'08		Oak		"
O	111	17'02		Oak		"
O	112	17'07		Oak		"
O	113	17'08		Oak		"
O	114	17'07		Oak		"
O	93	16'02		Oak		"
O	94	16'07		Oak		"
O	9S	16'03		Oak		"
O	148	20'03		Oak	Top left side of drive	"
O	370	15'02		Beech		"
O	371	15'03		Beech		"

Note: well over 20 Beech over 10'

Pri/Open	No.	Size	Feature	Type	Location	Map Ref.
O	312	15'05		Oak		"
O	313	15'02		Oak		"
O	315	14'03	*Dead*	Oak		"
O	314	14'09		Oak		"
					(Odds)	
O	317	17'03		Oak	Woods?	"
O	6	14'00		Wellingtonia		"
O	349	19'06	*Arch, hollow*	Oak	Near New Bam Wood	"
O	311	18'00		Oak	Field below house	"
O	7	14'01		Sweet Chestnut	?	"
O	110	17'10	*35' base*	Sweet Chestnut	Near house	"
O	374	17'09		Wellingtonia		"
O	318	16'09		Oak	Wood?	"
O	372	14'09		Wellingtonia		"
O	373	14'08		Wellingtonia		"
O	394	14'01		Oak	Next to main wall	"
O	369	14'00		Oak	Near top gate house	"
O	8	14'01		Lawson Cypress	?	"
O	350	14'02	*Very tall*	Beech		"
O	348	14'00	*Nearly dead*	Oak		"
O	393	14'10		Oak	Next to deer fence	"
O	368	U/O		Lime	Next to top gatehouse	"

Long Ashton

Ashton Hill Plantation

Pri/Open	No.	Size	Feature	Type	Location	Map Ref.
O	195	20'06		Wellingtonia	Ashton Hill Plantation	70/52
O	196	20'09		"	"	"
O	202	19'05		"	"	"
O	193	21'06		"	"	"
O	199	19'11		"	"	"
O	200	19'04		"	"	"
O	197	20'09		"	"	"
O	201	19'03		"	"	"
O	215	16'07		"	"	"
O	216	16'00		"	"	"
O	229	15'06		"	"	"
O	220	16'03		"	"	"
O	218	16'09		"	"	"
O	211	17'10		"	"	"
O	221	16'10		"	"	"
O	206	18'07		"	"	"
O	198	20'07		"	"	"
O	217	16'03		"	"	"
O	219	16'10		"	"	"
O	222	16'11		"	"	"
O	209	17'04		"	"	"
O	223	16'08		"	"	"
O	224	16'09		"	"	"
O	228	15'08		"	"	"
O	225	16'02		"	"	"
O	226	16'05		"	"	"
O	227	15'07		"	"	"
O	210	17'03		"	"	"
O	214	16'00		"	"	"
O	204	18'07		"	"	"
O	207	19'0S		"	"	"
O	205	18'07		"	"	"

Note: 35 wellingtonias planted by Sir John Smyth of Ashton Court after 1838. 32 planted together.

Many thanks to Bob Cook

Loxton

Christon

Hamwood Park

Over thirty beech trees over 10'00, four over 14'00. Beech trees from Hamwood park were taken to France and used for the Mulberry Landings in the second world war. Single trunk Ash 18'02 on the lane going to the Gortons.

Five oaks in the field next to the Old Rectory, not pollarded. They can be seen from the road. Private property.

In The Car

See Wincombe Parish, Barton

On Foot

West Mendip Way

Banwell Hill

Locking Church

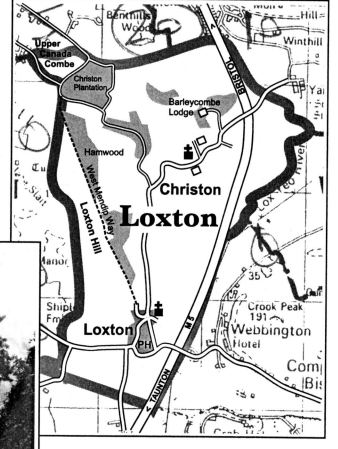

"Superb views while walking the West Mendip Way"

Ash – Ref: 166, 18'02 - Single Trunk The Gortons, Christon

Loxton Parish   Loxton

Pri/Open	No.	Size	Feature	Type	Location	Map Ref.
O	1445	15'01	*Bluebells everywhere*	Beech	Loxton Hill Woods, top part	56/37
O	1446	14'11		Beech	"	"
O	1447	14'07		Beech	"	"
P	1448	U/O	*Ancient wall*	Ash	Loxton woods	
P	1486	14'00	*Ancient bank*	Katies Ash	Small wood above Westhill House	
P	1487	M/T	*Ancient bank*	Field Maple	"	"

Loxton Parish   Christon

Pri/Open	No.	Size	Feature	Type	Location	Map Ref.
P	165	19'05		Oak	Field next to Old Rectory	57/37
P	168	16'07		Oak	"	"
P	169	16'02		Oak	"	"
P	171	15'07		Oak	"	"
P	172	15'07		Oak	"	"
P	167	17'05		Oak	Oakes Farm	56/37
P	170	16'10		Oak	"	"
P	173	15'02		Oak	"	"
P	179	U/O		Lime	Old Rectory	57/37
P	180	U/O		Lime	"	"
P	181	U/O		Lime	"	"
0	166	18'02		Ash	Lane to the Gortons	"
P	174	14'00		Beech	Hamwood Park	"
P	175	14'00		Beech	"	"
P	176	14'02		Beech	"	"
P	177	14'01		Beech	"	"

Note: Beech trees from Hamwood were used on the Mulberry landings in the 2nd World War.

Nailsea

There is a multi trunk yew (ref. 585) at Christ Church. 19'05 large pollarded Oak (ref. 1199) at Lodge Lane field

In The Car   Nailsea- Nailsea West End - Chelvey - Brockley Combe - Downside
Backwell Hill Road - Backwell Green - Backwell East End - Nailsea

On Foot   Clapton in Gordano - Brockley Church - Flax Bourton Church
Footpaths to Jacklands Bridge, Backwell Lake and Wraxall.

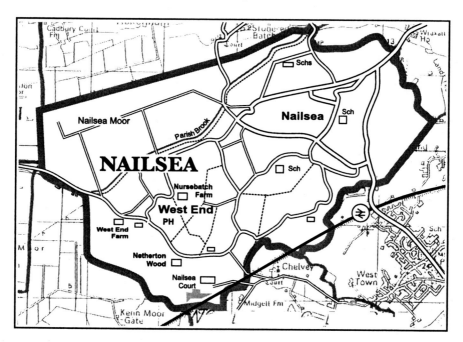

Nailsea

Pri/Open	No.	Size	Feature	Type	Location	Map Ref.
O	238	16'04		Oak	Youngwood Lane	69/46
P	189	14'07		Sweet Chestnut	Nailsea Court	68/45
P	239	14'07		Ash	Whiteoak House	69/48
P	585	M/T		Yew	Christ Church, Nailsea	70/42
O	1199	19'05		Oak	Field, Lodge Lane	70/48
O	1257	15'01	Triple trunk	Crack Willow	Main car park, Nailsea	70/47
O	1997	U/O	Ancient pollard	Ash	South of Nailsea Football Club	69/46
O	1998	U/O	"	Ash	"	"
O	1999	U/O	"	Ash	"	"
O	2000	U/O		Ash	PF, south of Nailsea Football Club	"
0	2001	U/O		Ash	"	"

Portbury

Over 50 ancient oaks over 10' from rifle range across to Honor Farm down the hill to Sheepgate Farm - was this an old estate?

20'6 huge oak tree growing to side of brook in field, Wharf Lane (ref. 194). This tree is huge. 27'3 multi trunk Ash (ref. 776) at Sheepgate Farm - both on private ground.

Was this part of Tyntesfield Estate?

In The Car

See Easton in Gordano

On Foot

Priors Wood

Birch Wood

Wraxall via Priors Wood

Easton in Gordano via Honor Farm and Halls Wood

Failand Hill House

Many thanks to

Mr & Mrs Voisey
and
Mr Lawson

Portbury

Pri/Open	No.	Size	Feature	Type	Location	Map Ref.
O	208	17'06		Yew	Portbury Church Yard	75/49
O	234	14'01	*Split trunk*	Yew	"	"
P	194	20'06		Oak	Field North of Wharf lane, next to brook	76/49
P	233	14'00		Willow	Springfield House	"
P	771	14'06	*Pollard*	Oak	Sheepgate Farm, field	75.76/48
P	772	14'00	"	Oak	"	"
P	773	14'10	"	Oak	Sheepgate Farm, next to old stone gate post	"
P	774	14'00		Oak	Sheepgate Farm, hedgerow	"
P	775	18'09	*Coppice*	Ash	"	"
P	776	27'03	"	Ash	"	"
			Long narrow multi-trunk (no public access)			
P	777	M/T	*Coppice*	Ash	Sheepgate Farm, hedgerow	
P	1088	16'04	*Pollard*	Oak	Oakham stream	74/50
P	1089	16'11	"	Oak	"	"
P	1090	16'08	"	Oak	"	"
P	1091	16'01	*8 trunks*	Ash	Oakham stream	
P	1092	U/O		Oak	"	"
P	1093	M/T	*10 trunks*	Alder	"	"
P	1094	14'09		Oak	Conygar Hill	75/ 49
P	1095	16'06	*25' at 10' up*	Oak	"	"
P	1096	14'10	*Split trunk*	Ash	"	"
P	1097	N/A		Oak	"	"
P	1098	N/A		Oak	"	"
P	1127	16'10		Oak	Honor Farm Wood	74/50
P	1128	U/O	*Crown collapsed*	Oak	"	"
					(plus another 10 ancient old pollards over 10')	
P	1129	14'02	*Split trunk*	Ash	"	"
P	1130	M/T	*4 trunks*	Ash	"	"
P	1428	N/A	Pollard	Oak	Field above Honor Farm	
P	1429	N/A	Pollard	Oak	"	"
P	1161	14'01		Oak	Pond, East of The Mount	75/50
P	1162	W/O	*Crown missing*	Oak	"	"
P	1163	14'03		Yew	Higher Farm Wood	"
P	1164	14'04		Yew	"	"
P	1165	14'03	*3 trunks, (base measure)*	Ash	"	"
P	1166	M/T		Ash	Higher Farm Wood	75/50
P	1167	15'04	*80' tall*	Sweet Chestnut	"	"

Portbury

Pri/Open	No.	Size	Feature	Type	Location	Map Ref.
P	1168	M/T	*Covered in ivy*	Oak	Old Ruin Small Wood	72/50
P	1169	14'03		Sweet Chestnut	Left side Porbury Lane	"
P	1170	17'03	*20' at 8' up (looking ill)*	Sweet Chestnut	PFP to the school	"
P	1171	M/T	*Coppice*	Hazel	Left Side Portbury Lane	"
P	1172	M/T	"	Hazel	"	"
P	1201	18'01	*6 trunks stool*	Ash	Portbury Lane Quarry Wood *(all old stools)*	
P	1202	14'03	*4 trunks stool*	Ash	"	"
P	1203	19'02	" *1 branch rooted*	Ash	"	"
P	1204	M/T	*Coppice*	Hazel	"	"
P	120S	M/T	*4 trunks*	Ash	"	"
P	1206	M/T	*3 trunks*	Ash	Portbury Lane Quarry Wood *(all old stools)*	72/50
P	1207	15'11	*11 trunks*	Ash	"	"
P	1208	M/T	*4 trunks*	Ash	"	"
P	1209	M/T	*6 trunks*	Oak	"	"
P	1430	14'07	*Stool measure*	Field Maple	Portubury Lane, Quarry Woods	"
P	1431	19'03	*5 trunks*	Field Maple	Portbury Lane, Quarry Woods, lower north side	"
P	1432	M/T	*3 trunks*	Oak	"	"
P	1433	M/T	*Coppice*	Hazel	"	"
P	1434	M/T	"	Hazel	"	"
O	1421	15'01	*Pollard*	Oak	Windmill Hill, near public foot path	73/50
O	1422	19'00		Oak	Ancient track - public footpath, Failand Lane to Windmill Hill	"
O	1423	17'10	*Lost one branch*	Oak	"	"
O	1424	U/O		Oak	"	"
O	142S	17'S		Oak	"	"
O	1426	14'07		Oak	"	"
P	1427	M/T	*Stool, 6 trunks*	Sweet Chestnut	Budding Wood	74/54
O	510	M/T	*Layered*	Sycamore	Caswell Hill	74/48
O	511	M/T	"	Sycamore	"	"
O	512	M/T	"	Sycamore	"	"

Note: Over 50 ancient Oaks over 10' from the rifle range across to Honour Farm, down the hill to Sheepgate Farm - was this an old estate?

Many thanks to Mr & Mrs Voisey, Mr Lawson

Portbury

Priors Wood, Public Foot Path Portbury Lodge and Old Rifle Range Fields)

Pri/Open	No.	Size	Feature	Type	Location	Map Ref.
O	1101	16'S	*Split trunk*	Ash	PFP, Portbury Lodge	74/49.50
O	1102	23'1	*4 trunks*	Sycamore	"	"
O	1103	148		Beech	Near PFP, Porbury Lodge	"
O	1104	26'4	*Layered m/t*	Field Maple	PFP, Portbury Lodge	"
O	1105	16'6	*5 trunks*	Ash	Track, Portbury Lodge	"
O	1106	14'10	*4 trunks*	Ash	"	"
O	1107	1 5'3	*3 trunks*	Ash	"	"
O	1108	14'09		Oak	Bullocks Bottom pond area, Priors Wood *(Wraxall Parish)*	"
O	1109	14'11	*5 trunks*	Ash	Priors Wood, South side	"
O	1110	14'03		Beech	"	"
O	1111	15'02	*Hollow, 5 trunks*	Ash	"	"
O	1112	14'09	*split*	Ash	"	"
O	1113	18'06	*4 trunks*	Ash	Priors Wood, East side	"
O	1114	16'07	*Not pollarded*	Oak	"	"
O	1115	18'02	*3 trunks*	Sweet Chestnut	"	"
O	1116	17'00	*5 trunks*	Sweet chestnut	"	"
O	1117	21'10	*7 trunks*	Sweet Chestnut	"	"
O	1118	14'00	*Split trunk*	Oak	Next to ditch, Priors Wood	
O	1119	U/O	"	Ash	"	"
P	1120	F/O	*Pollard*	Oak	Old rifle range	"
P	1121	F/O	"	Oak	"	"
P	1122	F/O	"	Oak	"	"
			(trunk split down middle)			
P	1123	F/O	"	Oak	"	"
P	1124	15'02	"	Oak	"	"
P	1125	15'10	"	Oak	"	"
P	1126	17'00	"	Oak	"	"
			(plus over 20 ancient oaks over 10')			
P	1067	16'00	*25' at 6' up*	Sweet Chestnut	Next to PFP from Birchwood	"

Portbury

Birchwood

Pri/Open	No.	Size	Feature	Type	Location	Map Ref.
O	1066	14'01		Yew	On PFP next to Birchwood Cottage	74/49
O	1068	M/T	*Pollard*	Sycamore	PF, Birchwood	"
O	1069	M/T	"	Sycamore	"	"
O	1070	M/T	"	Sycamore	"	"
O	1071	M/T	"	Ash	" "	"
P	1072	14'08	*6 trunks*	Sweet Chestnut	Left side looking up, Birchwood	"
P	1073	M/T	*3 trunks*	Sweet Chestnut	"	"
P	1074	M/T	*4 trunks*	Sweet Chestnut	"	"
P	1075	16'6	*5 trunks*	Sweet Chestnut	"	"
P	1076	15'3	*4 trunks*	Sweet Chestnut	"	"
P	1077	15'09	"	Sweet Chestnut	"	"
P	1078	16'04	"	Sweet Chestnut	"	"
P	1079	17'06	"	Sweet Chestnut	Birchwood, Top left	"
P	1080	16'00	*6 trunks*	Sweet Chestnut	"	"
P	1081	20'04	*4 trunks*	Sweet Chestnut	"	"
P	1082	14'10	*6 trunks*	Sweet Chestnut	"	"
P	1083	16'04	*4 trunks*	Sweet Chestnut	"	"
P	1084	14'06	*Single trunk*	Sweet Chestnut	Birchwood, Top right	"
P	1085	18'07	*Pollard*	Ash	"	"
P	1086	M/T	*Coppice*	Hazel	Birchwood, Top	"
P	1087	18'06	*Split trunk*	Sweet Chestnut	Nr Birchwood Cottage	"

Oak • Ref: 815 • Portishead Lake Car Park

Portishead

28'01 Lime (ref. 397) in Weston Big Wood.

Large 18'01 Oak (ref. 815) at Portishead Lake grounds.

On Foot

Weston Big Wood

Portishead to Clevedon Coastal Path

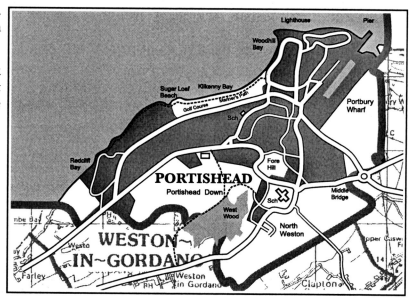

"Take the children, grand-children, grand-parents boating on Portishead Lake. There is also a café for refreshments"

Portishead

Pri/Open	No.	Size	Feature	Type	Location	Map Ref.
O	411	14'03		Cypress	Portishead Cemetry	75/46
O	397	28'01	*M/T pollard*	Lime	Weston Big Wood	75/45
O	398	M/T		Lime	"	"
O	399	M/T		Lime	"	"
O	400	M/T		Lime	"	"
O	401	M/T		Ash	"	"
O	402	19'07	*7 trunks*	Ash	"	"
O	403	17'09	*4 trunks*	Ash	"	"
O	404	18'02	*4 trunks*	Lime	"	"
O	40S	M/T		Lime	"	"
O	406	17'00	*5 trunks*	Lime	"	"
O	407	19'08	*5 trunks*	Lime	Weston Big Wood, near stream	"
O	408	15'02		Lime	"	"
O	409	17'03		Lime	"	"
O	410	15'02		Lime	"	"
P	812	M/T	*6 trunks*	Sycamore	Portishead Dock	77/47
O	813	16'06		Ash	East Wood	"
P	814	20'03		Sweet Chestnut	"	"
0	815	18'01	*Huge, spreading*	Oak	Portishead Lake grounds	77/46

Sandford

15'10 Beech at Sandford Church (ref. 56). Quite a few old Hazel coppices at Sandford quarry.

Sandford Wood - **BEWARE OPEN MINE-SHAFTS - NO CHILDREN, NO PETS**

In The Car   See Winscombe

On Foot   Sandford Hill and on to Star
Limestone Link

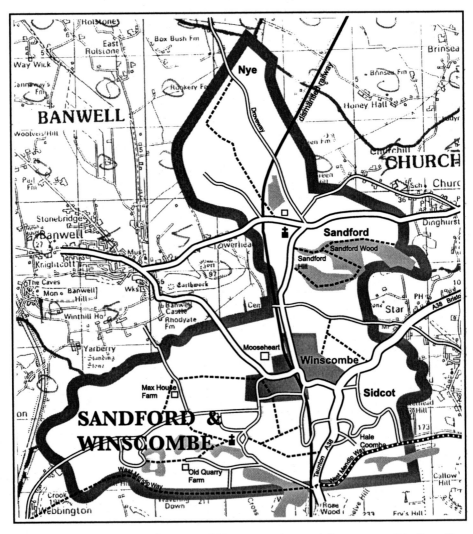

"Look out for Sandford's famous 50' orange tree at Avoncrop, Station Road."

Sandford

Pri/Open	No.	Size	Feature	Type	Location	Map Ref.
O	56	15'10	Beech		Sandford Churchyard	59/42
O	574	M/T	*Old coppice*	Hazel	Sandford Quarry	58/42
O	575	M/T	"	Hazel	Near public footpath	"
P	14SS	15'00		Lime	Lyncombe Woods, bottom right	59/43
P	1456	15'05	*Old bottle in trunk*	Lime	" top left	"
P	1457	M/T		Lime	"	"
P	14S8	M/T		Lime	"	"
P	1459	M/T		Lime	"	"
P	1460	M/T		Lime	"	"
P	1461	M/T		Lime	"	"
P	1462	M/T		Lime	"	"
P	1463	M/T		Lime	"	"
P	1464	M/T		Lime	"	"
P	1465	M/T		Lime	"	"
P	1466	M/T		Lime	"	"
P	1467	16'00		Parish boundary Lime	" top left	"
O	1780	17'04		Wellingtonia	Droveway railway bridge *	60/41
O	X	12'04	Wellingtonia	Wellingtonia	" *	"

* Were these two trees planted at the same time as this bridge was built?

P	1781	15'04	*Hollow*	Oak	Field north of Willetts Yard	"

Sandford Wood   Note: Beware mine shafts No children - No pets

P	1717	M/T	*Hole through middle*	Ash	Sandford wood	59/42
P	1718	D/T		Lime	"	"
P	1719	18'10	*Stool*	Lime	"	"
P	1720	17'10	"	Lime	"	"
P	1721	15'08	"	Lime	"	"
P	1722	14'00	"	Lime	"	"
P	1723	14'05	"	Lime	"	"
P	1724	M/T	"	Lime	"	"
P	1725	M/T	"	Lime	Sandford wood	59/42
P	1726	M/T	"	Lime	"	"
P	1727	M/T	"	Lime	"	"
P	1728	M/T	"	Lime	"	"
P	1729	M/T	"	Lime	"	"
P	1730	U/O	*Fallen, still growing*	Lime	"	"
P	1731	M/T		Ash	"	"
P	1732	M/T		Ash	"	"
P	1733	MIT	*Stool, on outcrop*	Oak	"	"
O	1734	M/T	*Layered*	Ash	Public foot path below Sandford Wood	"
O	1735	14'02	20'+ at l0'	Oak	"	"
O	1736	14'01	*Huge*	Ash	Hedgerow below Sandford Wood	"
O	1737	N/A		Lime	"	"

Tickenham

Long narrow S trunk Lime 25'7 (ref. 1819).

Very large single trunk Oak 21'00 (ref. 1818), hedgerow below Summer House Wood.

24'00 single trunk Lime at Fully Farm (ref. 6S2) - this has been fenced off and looked after by Stuart Plant.

There is a Cedar planted in Tickenham House by Edward VII when he used to come to Bristol to see Lady Smythe. This tree is not registered as it is not 14'00.

On Foot   Across the footbridge to Clevedon - Lime Breach Wood
Cadbury Camp

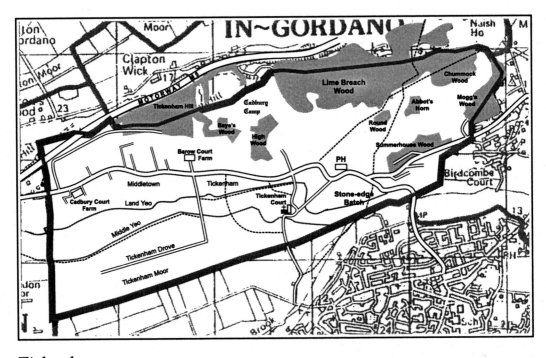

Tickenham

Pri/Open	No.	Size	Feature	Type	Location	Map Ref.
					Tickenham House Area (Built 1730)	
P	1025	17'00		Horse Chestnut	New drive to barn	72/47
P	1026	14'09	*Pollard*	Lime	Field east of house	"
P	1027	14'01	"	Lime	"	"
P	1028	M/T	"	Lime	"	"
P	1029	M/T	"	Lime	The Limes, east of house	"
P	1030	M/T	"	Lime	"	"
P	1031	M/T	"	Lime	"	"

Many thanks to: John Strode, Tickenham House & Stewart Plant, Tickenham Court

Tickenham

Pri/Open	No.	Size	Feature	Type	Location	Map Ref.
O	586	W/O		Willow	Jacklands Fish Farm on Parish Brook	72/47
O	587	W/O		Willow	"	"
O	600	27'00	Nesting box	Lime	High Wood (no public access)	72/48
O	601	19'00	2 trunks	Lime	High Wood, top part by stile	"
O	602	19'00	8 trunks	Lime	High Wood, middle part	"
O	603-650			Lime	47 in total, all Limes growing from ancient stools, all in High Wood	"
P	652	24'01	Single trunk	Lime	Fully Farm (no public access)	72/45
O	6S3	20'06	4 trunks	Lime	Fully Farm, bridle path	"
O	700	14'10	Split trunk	Oak	"	"
P	1049	14'01		Oak	Chummock Wood	72/47
P	1050	18'01	5 trunks	Oak	"	"
P	1051	18'00		Oak	"	"
P	10S2	M/T	Stool	Small Leaf Lime	"	"
P	1053	M/T	Stool	Small Leaf Lime	"	"
P	1054	14'09	5 trunks	Oak	"	"
P	1800	17'10	4 trunks	Oak	Old Lane, next to Lime Burner	72/46
P	1801	M/T	Stool	Ash	"	"
P	1802	M/T	Stool	Ash	"	"
P	1803	15'04	4 trunks	Ash	Old Lane, Old Wood	"
P	1804	M/T	3 trunks	Ash	"	"
P	1805	MIT	3 trunks	Ash	"	"
O	1806	MIT	5 trunks	Ash	Old Lane, above Old Wood	"
P	1807	MIT	3 trunks (old stool)	Ash	Old Lane, Abbots Horn Wood	"
P	1808	M/T	3 trunks	Ash	"	"
P	1809	M/T	3 trunks (old stool)	Ash	Old Lane, Abbots Hom Wood	72/46
P	1810	M/T	3 trunks	Ash	"	"
P	1811		Decayed trunk	Ash	"	"
P	1812	21'03	"	Lime	"	"
P	1813		"	Lime	"	"
P	1814	14'03	3 trunks	Ash	"	"
P	181S	M/T	4 trunks	Ash	"	"
P	1816	20'04	Stool	Ash	"	"
P	1817	17'05	6 trunks	Ash	"	"
P	1818	21'00	Single trunk	Oak	Hedgerow below Summerhouse Wood	"
P	1819	25'07	5 trunks, long narrow trunk	Lime	"	"
O	1834		Single trunk, decayed	Ash	Bayes Wood above Old Quarry	72/45

Cadbury Camp - nothing of any size

Tickenham

Pri/Open	No.	Size	Feature	Type	Location	Map Ref.
P	1823	M/T		Sycamore	Moggs Wood above pylon	72/47
P	1824	15'07	6 trunks	Sycamore	"	"
P	1825	14'03		Oak	"	"
P	1826	15'02	2 trunks	Sweet Chestnut	Moggs Wood below pylon (all stools)	"
P	1827	19'07	4 trunks	Sweet Chestnut	"	"
P	1828	18'06	4 trunks	Sweet Chestnut	"	"
P	1829	18'07	7 trunks	Sweet Chestnut	"	"
P	1830	17'08	5 trunks	Sweet Chestnut	"	"
P	1831	M/T	5 trunks	Sweet Chestnut	"	"
P	1833	M/T	5 trunks	Sweet Chestnut	"	"
P	1832	15'00	Dead trunk	???	"	"
P	1097	15'00	Single trunk	Oak	Summer House Wood all ancient stools	72/46
P	1908	M/T		Lime	"	"
P	1909	14'00	3 trunks	Ash	"	"
P	1910	14'00	3 trunks	Ash	"	"
P	1911	14'06	4 trunks	Ash	"	"
P	1912	M/T		Lime	"	"
P	1913	18'00	4 trunks	Ash	"	"
P	1914	16'00	7 trunks	Ash	"	"
P	1915	M/T		Ash	"	"
P	1916	17'00	5 trunks, base measure	Ash	"	"
P	1917	21'	4 trunks	Ash	"	"
P	1918	1 6'8		Horse Chestnut	"	"
					Lime Breach Woods	
P	1835	M/T	Stool	Sweet Chestnut	"	72/45.46
P	1836	M/T	"	Sweet Chestnut	"	"
P	1837	M/T	"	Sweet Chestnut	"	"
P	1838	M/T	"	Sweet Chestnut	"	"
P	1839	16'03	"	Oak	"	"
P	1840	14'04	"	Oak	"	"
P	1841	14'00	"	Ash	Lower boundary	"
P	1842	U/O	"	Lime	"	"
P	1843	U/O	"	Ash	"	"
P	1844	14'02	"	Lime	"	"
P	1845	14'00	"	Ash	"	"
P	1846	14'08	"	Lime	"	"
P	1847	16'00	"	Lime	"	"
P	1848	17'07	"	Lime	"	"
P	1849	16'06	"	Lime	"	"
P	1850	1T2	Split	lime	"	"
P	1851	17'04	Stool	Lime	Old Lane, public footpath	"
P	1852-1890		All multi trunk old Lime stools, last cut 1948-1950			

Many thanks to: Matthew Bryant

Walton in Gordano

Manor House

20'10 Plane, 100' (ref. 798) at the Manor House. Many thanks to Mr & Mrs S M Wills. Private ground.

7 trees over 14'00 at Manor House fields. Private ground but trees can be seen from main road.

Walton Common

No trees over 14' that I could find in this area There are quite a few ancient Yews, one over 13' growing out of the side of rocks. Very good walking and views.

Walton in Gordano

Pri/Open	No.	Size	Feature	Type	Location	Map Ref.
P	798	20'10	*100' high*	Plane	Manor House	73/42
P	799	14'08	*80' high*	Lime	Manor House (old avenue - last Lime left)	"
P	***	12'00		Monkey Puzzle	"	"
P	805	16'02	*20'+ at base*	Lime	Manor House fields	"
P	806	18'01		Oak	Near footpath, Manor House fields	"
P	807	17'03	*Pollard*	Horse Chestnut	"	"
P	808	14'04	"	Lime	" (Group of	"
P	809	14'02	"	Lime	" five, other two	"
P	810	14'00	"	Lime	" under 14')	"
P	811	14;05	*Split trunk*	Lime	" (on it's own)	"
O	1061	M/T	*Old stool*	Ash	Next to footpath, Rock Woods	"
O	1062	M/T	"	Ash	Next to wall, Rock Woods	"
O	1063	17'01	"	Beech	Rock Woods *(storm damaged)*	"
O	1064	14'04		Beech	"	"
O	1065	U/O		Beech	Rock Woods *(huge, blown over)*	"

Many thanks to Mr & Mrs S M Wills

Limes • Ref: 808 -811 • Manor House Fields, Walton in Gordano

Weston in Gordano

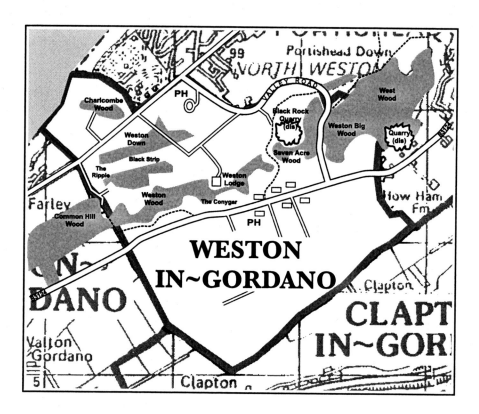

Weston in Gordano

Pri/Open	No.	Size	Feature	Type	Location	Map Ref.
P	1791	14'03	*4 trunks*	Oak	Seven Acre Wood	74/44
P	1792	M/T		Sweet Chestnut	Weston Lodge Wood	"
P	1793	M/T	*10 trunks plus*	Oak	"	"
P	1794	M/T		Oak	"	"
P	179S	15'10	*Triple trunk*	Oak	"	"
P	1796	M/T		Ash	"	"
P	1797	M/T		Ash	"	"
O	1798	B/O	*Large single branch, unable to measure*	Oak	Public footpath, Weston Wood East	"

Weston super Mare

15'09 split trunk HolmITurkey Oak at Lodge Drive, part of old Miller-Barstow Estate.

Nothing else of any size in Weston super Mare - Weston woods are fairly new, planted in the last 200 years. There was a Cypress which was cut down in 2002 - I do not understand why this tree was cut down when it could have been pollarded or thinned out as there are very few large trees in Weston super Mare.

Walks - Weston Woods, Monks Step

Worle	15'11 Willow at Apple Tree Farm, Ebdon Road (ref. 765) - private property. 14'00 Cypress at St Martins Church yard (ref. 702). Walks - Worle Hill Observatory. River Banwell Walk
Oldmixon	15'11 Willow (ref. 764) at Gazelle Road. Walks - Footpath from Oldmixon to Bleadon through Hay Wood and onto West Mendip Way.
Uphill	16'06 Beech (ref. 73) at Uphill Donkey Field
In the Car	Weston super Mare - Uphill Village - Bleadon Village - Loxton Cross - Axbridge - Cheddar - Wedmore - Wells -Wookey Hole Priddy - Cheddar Gorge - Winscombe - Weston super Mare
On Foot	Walk up to Uphill Church on the Hill Good food at the Ship Inn, Uphill Along the beach from Uphill to Weston or vice versa Ferry to Brean Down from Uphill (summer only) West Mendip Way

"Weston Museum is well worth a visit on a rainy day"

Weston super Mare

Pri/Open	No.	Size	Feature	Type	Location	Map Ref.
P	178	1 5'9	*Split trunk*	Holm Turkey Oak	Oak Lodge Drive, Old Barstow Estate "	62/42 "
P	199	M/T		Cypress	Upper Bristol Road	"
O	766	W/O	Pollard	Willow	Moor Lane	61/35

Weston Woods	Nothing over 14ft
Ashcombe Park	"
Grove Park	"

"Springtime – See the daffodils in Grove Park and snowdrops in Uphill Donkey Field"

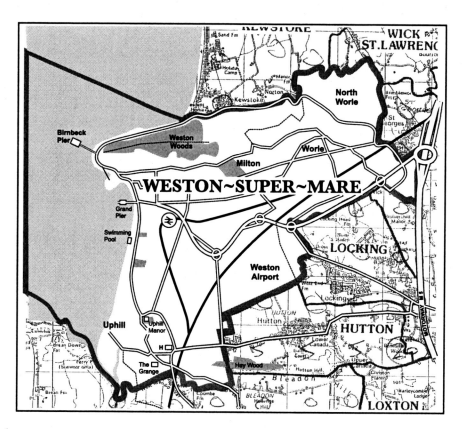

Worle

Pri/Open	No.	Size	Feature	Type	Location	Map Ref.
O	702	14'00		Cypress	St Martins Churchyard	63/35
P	765	15'11	*Pollard*	Willow	Apple Tree Farm, Ebdon Road	63/36

Oldmixon

Pri/Open	No.	Size	Feature	Type	Location	Map Ref.
O	764	15'11	Pollard	Willow	Gazelle Road	58/33
P	848	14'02		Beech	Hay Wood, West	58/34
P	849	MIT	Split	Oak	"	"
P	8S0	MIT	Coppice	Ash	"	"

Uphill

Pri/Open	No.	Size	Feature	Type	Location	Map Ref.
O	2	14'03		Horse Chestnut	Donkey Field	58/31
O	3	14'02		Beech	"	"
O	73	16'6		Beech	"	"

*"Remains of metal railings in an oak tree in the car park entrance of Grove Park —
this was caused by a German bomb. The oak is not referenced as it is under 14'."*

Wick St Lawrence

Magnificent split trunk Cedar (ref. 703) at The Cedars, many thanks to Mr & Mrs John Parsons. Private property.

14'00 Yew in Church yard (ref. 701).

The Cedars — Ref: 703

Wick St Lawrence

Pri/Open	No.	Size	Feature	Type	Location	Map Ref.
P	703	1 8'05	Split	Cedar	The Cedars	65/36
0	701	14'00		Yew	Church yard	"

Many thanks to Mr John Parsons.

Winford

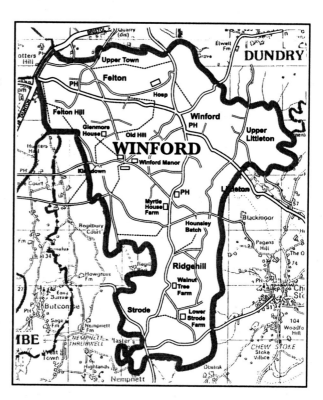

There is a large Beech (ref. 1514)   at Winford Manor, Bird Farm

On Foot
Monarch Way

Public Foot Paths
Meade Farm to East Dundry (Bit of a climb)
Winford Manor to Felton Common

Winford

Pri/Open	No.	Size	Feature	Type	Location	Map Ref.
O	1510	16'05		Beech	Crossroads, Winford Manor	65/54
P	1511	16'10		Beech	Winford Manor	"
P	1512	15'02	*Pollard*	Sweet Chestnut	"	"
P	1513	14'01		Beech	"	"
P	1514	18'08		Beech	Bird Farm, Winford Manor	"
P	1515	16'00		Beech	"	"
O	1516	17'04	*20' + base, single trunk*	Ash	Field next to Old Hill, near Winford Manor	
O	1517	14'08	*Growing on a hump*	Oak	Public footpath, Winford to Crown Hill	"
P	1706	1 4'01		Oak	Aquaduct hedgerow	"
O	1707	M/T		Ash	Spring Farm bridle way	"
O	1708	M/T		Ash	"	"
O	1709	M/T		Ash	"	"
O	1710	M/T		Field Maple	"	"
P	1711	U/O		Ash	The Willows, Regil Road	"

Note: Pink primroses growing in Winford

Winscombe

20'00 ancient Yew at Winscombe Church. An even larger Yew at the Old Rectory, 22'10 (ref. 673) which has been bashed about a bit. Very large Sycamore 16'03 (ref. 687) on Barton Drove which was damaged by a whirlwind in 1999.

15'01 (ref. 720) Sycamore in Broad/Church Knoll woods. 19'08 very old pollarded Ash with 6 trunks on an old drove above the Church.

Winscombe Hall   21'03 (ref. 788) Beech - 30'00 + at 8ft above ground. Largest Beech in North Somerset that I can find.

A 16'10 Fern Beech (ref. 791) is the only Fern Beech over 14'00 that I have found in the whole of North Somerset. Private property.

Nut Tree Farm   21'02 old pollarded Alder (ref. 1037) - it's huge. Ask John Mabbet (farmer) for permission to view and take wellingtons, wet ground.

Sidcot   Large Horse Chestnut 17'02 (ref. 1059)

Barton   There is a 17'09 Beech in Barton Rock grounds. You can see this tree from the public footpath. There is also a very old coppiced ash at 1 6'4 (ref. 677) on a public footpath above Longacre. Many ancient Hazel coppices along Barton Drove.

In the Car   Winscombe - Barton - Webbington - Cross - Axbridge
Cheddar Gorge - Miners Arms, Wells - Wookey Hole
Priddy - Charterhouse - Shipham - Winscombe

On Foot   Railway walk Winscombe to Sandford
Railway walk Winscombe to Cheddar
Winscombe to Barton
Footpath from Winscombe to Wavering Down
West Mendip Way
Banwell Castle
From Sidcot to Lilypool Cafe (nice cup of tea), public foot path
Lilypool Cafe to the Woodborough Pub for a Sunday dinner
Sidcott Spring Walk to Shipham
Barton Drove to Winscombe Church
Cross (good food at the White Hart)
Crooks Peak

"Take the children and grand-children safely on their bikes to Cheddar along the Railway Walk and see the stalagtites in Winscombe Tunnel"

For Map of Parish see Sandford Page 72

Ancient Yew, Winscombe Church — Ref: 674

Winscombe

Pri/Open	No.	Size	Feature	Type	Location	Map Ref.
P	78	16'09		Wellingtonia	Westhanger Lane	56/42
P	135	19'04		Wellingtonia	"	"
P	126	18'03		Wellingtonia	"	"
P	106	17'03		Wellingtonia	"	"
P	107	17'04		Cypress	"	"
P	61	15'00		Cypress	"	"
P	19	14'00		Cypress	"	"
P	89	16'04		Beech	"	"
P	116	18'11		Wellingtonia	Moose Hall	57/41
P	769	14'00		Oak	North of Moose Hall next to small pond	"
P	770	15'00	*Split trunk*	Willow	North of Moose Hall next to public footpath	
P	673	22'10		Yew	Church, house (no public access)	
P	674	20'00		Yew	Church grounds	
O	687	16'03	*Damaged by whirlwind*	Sycamore	Barton Drove	56/40.41
O	686	15'00		Oak	"	"
O	684	14'02	M/T	Field Maple	"	"
P	78	16'09		Wellingtonia	A38	56/42
O	681	M/T	*Coppice*	Hazel	"	"
O	682	M/T	"	Hazel	"	"
O	685	14'10		Ash	"	"
P	683	16'00	*Pollard*	Ash	Old Quarry Farm, Barton Dove	"

Winscombe

Pri/Open	No.	Size	Feature	Type	Location	Map Ref.
P	18	14'01		Wellingtonia	Furcroft, Barton Road	56/41
O	573	14'03		Oak	Next to Orchard, Shipham Lane	"
P	108	17'02		Cypress	Wyvem House, Church Road, next to stream	"
0	716	16'09		Beech	The Orchard	"
O	717	14'00	4 trunks	Field Maple	"	"
O	725	M/T	Coppice	Lime	Broad/Church Knoll Woods	56/40.41
O	718	17'00	Holly	Beech	"	"
O	719	15'00	Split trunk	Ash	"	"
O	720	15'01		Sycamore	"	"
O	722	15'03	4 trunks	Ash	"	"
O	723	0	2 trunks	Ash	"	"
O	724	16'00	Split	Oak	"	"
O	721	19'08	6 trunks	Ash	Old Drove above limage	56/40
			(3 trunks upright 3 blown over. Very old pollard)			
O	935	15'06	Concrete post	Oak	Field, North Eastwell Lane	56/41
O	920	14'08	Barbed wire	Oak	Hedgerow, North Eastwell lane	"
O	963	15'08		Oak	Cricket Pitch, top left	"
O	964	U/O		Oak	Rugby Pitch, left side	"
O	965	U/O		Oak	"	"
P	966	U/O		Oak	Hedgerow, Fullers Lane	"
P	967	14'00		Oak	"	"
P	968	U/O	Old pollard	Ash	Next to pond, Fullers Lane	"
O	1341	16'10	"	Oak	Yadley Lane, top part	56/42
O	1342	16'10		Oak	"	"
P	1449	14'04	Split	Ash	The Avenue	57/43
P	1450	18'05	Split	Oak	South of The Avenue, hedgerow	"
P	1451	14'10	Split	Oak	"	"
P	1452	14'02		Beech	" field	"
P	14S3	17'00		Ash	" hedgerow	"
0	1454	20'06	Huge, not pollarded	Oak	Public foot path, south of Winterhead	"
P	1782	M/T		Tulip Tree	Sidcott Lane	57/42
P	1974	U/O		Cypress	Hillyfields, White Stone Cottage	"
O	1975	U/O	Single trunk, hairy base	Sycamore	Puplic footpath, Paddingham House	57/43
O	1976	U/O	Layered	Sycamore	"	"
O	1977	20'8	Very large stump	Ash	Hedgerow, north east of Paddingham house	57/42
O	1978	U/O	Split	Ash	"	"
O	1979	U/O	Pollard	Ash	Public footpath, Max House Farm	57/41

Many thanks to Colonel Lewis

Winscombe   Winscombe Hall (Built 1859)

Pri/Open	No.	Size	Feature	Type	Location	Map Ref.
P	785	15'08	*Split trunk*	Holm/Turkey Oak	Main drive	56/41
P	786	15'09	*3 trunks*	"	"	"
P	787	14'00		"	"	"
P	788	21'03	*30' at 6' up*	Beech	West of Hall	"
P	789	16'00	*6 trunks*	Beech	"	"
P	790	15'02	*3 trunks*	Beech	"	"
P	791	16'10	*Split*	Fern Beech *	Main drive	"
P	792	14'02	*5 trunks*	Beech	"	"
P	793	21'00	*4 trunks*	Beech	Below Hall (no public access)	"
P	794	14'09	M/T	Beech	"	"
P	795	19'00	M/T	Beech	"	"
P	796	14'07	M/T	Copper Beech	"	"

*   The only Fern Beech over 14'00 found in North Somerset

Winscombe   Nut Tree Farm (Pre 1799)

Pri/Open	No.	Size	Feature	Type	Location	Map Ref.
P	1032	15'00	*Twin headed*	Oak	Field, South, (no public access)	57/41
P	1033	17'08	*Huge*	Oak	"	"
P	1034	15'02	*New tree house*	Oak	Winscombe brook, (no public access)	"
P	1035	15'04	*Old tree house*	Oak	"	"
P	1036	U/O		Willow	"	"
P	1037	21'02	*Old pollard*	Alder	"	"
P	1038	M/T	*3trunks*	Alder	"	"
P	1039	W/O		Alder	"	"
P	1040	W/O		Alder	"	"
P	1041	W/O		Sycamore	"	"

Many thanks to John Mabbett

Winscombe — Sidcot

Pri/Open	No.	Size	Feature	Type	Location	Map Ref.
O	1055	14'01		Lime	PFP to Sidcott spring	57/42.43
O	1056	15'00		Beech	"	"
O	1057	15'06		Lime	"	"
O	1058	16'00		Beech	"	"
O	1059	17'02		Horse Chestnut	"	"
O	1060	15'00	*Pollard, 7 trunks*	Lime	"	"
O	n/a	10'04		Tree of Heaven	Hillyfields	"
P	1891	M/T		Hornbeam	Elmside, Bridgwater Road	"
P	1892	M/T		Hornbeam	"	"

Winscombe — Barton

Pri/Open	No.	Size	Feature	Type	Location	Map Ref.
P	674	17'09		Beech	Barton Rocks grounds	56/39.40
P	675	15'05		Beech	"	"
P	676	14'02		Beech	"	"
O	677	16'04	*Coppice 4 trunks*	Ash	Wood above Long Acre, Barton Hill	"
O	678	14'03		Oak	Old Road to Barton Rocks	"
O	679	M/T		Hazel	Public footpath above Barton Rocks	"
O	680	M/T		Hazel	"	"
O	1755	17'06		Ash	Shute Shelve Wood	"
O	1756	M/T		Oak	"	"
O	1757	M/T	*Split*	Oak	"	"
O	1758	14'03		Ash	"	"
O	1759	M/T	*Stool*	Lime	"	"
O	1760	M/T	"	Lime	"	"
O	1761	M/T	*Collapsed*	Lime	"	"
O	n/a	11'07	*80' tall*	Field Maple	"	"
P	1762	15'01	*Spreading*	Oak	Old drove north of Shute Shelve Wood	"
P	1763	14'9		Oak	"	"
O	1778	21 '04	*8 trunk stool*	Sycamore	Public foot path, Gatcombe House to Sidcott	"
P	1779	N/A		Ash	Winterhead Farm	"

Wraxall

Tyntesfield Estate

Late Lord Wraxall kept the trees on his estate in excellent order and had a great interest in trees. Huge Beech 21'02 (ref. 891) next to house. Wellingtonia, 26'04 (ref. 898), 4th largest Wellingtonia in North Somerset. There are also Lime avenues, most of which are under 14'00 but look superb in May.

Downs School Area

Three Luncombe Oaks (ref. 1180, 1181 and 1182). Large 16'00 Lime (ref. 1176) with huge L shaped bough at least 10'00 in circumference. A magnificent 16'03 Copper Beech (ref. 513)

Failand Hill House

Wellingtonia, 28'00 (ref. 659), 3rd largest in North Somerset

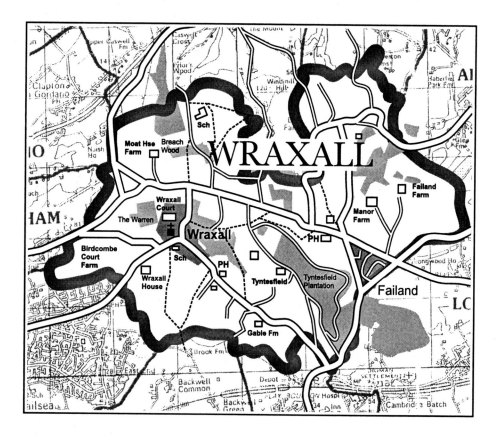

Wraxall

Pri/Open	No.	Size	Feature	Type	Location	Map Ref.
O	512	15'07		Yew	Wraxall Church Yard	71/49
O	578	14'01		Oak	Towerhouse Wood, bottom	"
O	579	M/T	5 trunks	Ash	"　　next to stream	"
O	580	M/T	18'+	Lime	"　　next to foot path	"
O	581	M/T		Sweet Chestnut	"　　middle	"
O	582	M/T		Sweet Chestnut	"　　middle	"
O	583	X	Lost in gales 2001	Oak	"　　bottom	"
O	584	W/O		Ash	"　　next to stream	"
P	563	18'06		Wellingtonia	Bath Wood	"
P	564	16'04		Wellingtonia	Barton Rocks grounds	56/39.40
P	565	W/O		Ash	"　, next to stream	"
P	566	W/O		Lime	"　, next to stream	"
O	991	16'	5 trunk stool	Oak	Weir Lane, south east, Mulberry Farm	73/52
O	992	M/T	4 trunks	Ash	"	"
O	993	16'3	Pollard	Ash	Field next to public footpath, south of Weir Lane	"
O	994	M/T	Coppice	Hazel	Ferney Row, Gordano Way, public foot path	
O	995	M/T	Coppice	Hazel	"	"
O	996	15'09	Pollard	Ash	"	"
O	997	19'04	Dead pollard	Oak	West side of Ox House Bottom Wood	"
O	998	14'06	4 trunks	Ash	Public foot path, Ox House Bottom Wood	"
O	999	16'02		Oak	Spring near Ox House Bottom Wood	"
P	1000	14'06	Pollard	Ash	Very small wood north of Failand Farm	72/52
P	1200	15'04	20'+ at 10' up	H/Chestnut	Field north of Limekiln Plantation	75/50
P	1893	17'05	Split	H/Chestnut	Wraxall Manor House	
P	1894	M/T	Stool	Alder	Cradle Bridge area	71/48
P	1895	M/T	Stool	Alder	"	"
P	1896	M/T	Stool	Alder	"	"
P	1897	M/T	Stool	Alder	"	"
P	1898	M/T	Stool	Alder	"	"
P	1899	M/IT		Ash	Hedgerow east of Manor House	71/49
P	1900	D/T		Ash	"	"
P	1901	U/O	Bulbous	Ash	"	"
O	1902	14'02		Oak	Public footpath, Brook Farm to Wraxall Church (hedgerow)	71/48
O	1903	14'03		Oak	Public footpath, Brook Farm to Wraxall Church　(field)	71/48
O	1904	20'00		Oak	"　(hedgerow)	"
O	1905	U/O		Oak	"　(hedgerow)	"
P	1906	W/O	25' at 10'	Willow	Ditch south of Wraxall School	"
P	1907	U/C		Oak	Hedgerow, east of Pastures pond	"

Wraxall

Pri/Open	No.	Size	Feature	Type	Location	Map Ref.
O	512	15'07		Yew	Wraxall Church Yard	71/49
P	1908	M/T	Stool	Alder	Pastures pond	"
P	1909	16'01	Base measure, split	Oak	Hedgerow next to football pitch	71/49
P	1910	U/O		Oak	Next to Northampton House	"
P	1911	15'04	L shaped	H/Chestnut	Watercress Farm	70/49
P	1912	W/O		Alder	Watercress Farm brook	"
P	1913	W/O		Alder	"	"
P	1914	W/O		Alder	"	"
P	1915	W/O		Alder	"	"
P	1916	M/T		Alder	Copse east of Watercress Farm	"
P	1917	M/T		Alder	"	"
P	1918	M/T		Alder	"	"
P	1919	M/T		Alder	"	"
P	1923	W/O		Willow	Watercress spring	70/50
P	1924	W/O		Willow	"	"
P	1925	14'07		H/Chestnut	"	"
P	1926	14'07	Stump	Field Maple	Farm track Gable Farm	"

Wraxall Court

Pri/Open	No.	Size	Feature	Type	Location	Map Ref.
P	1956	14'00		Lime		72/48
P	1955	15'08		Lime		
P	1960	18'00		Beech	Cut down Jan 2002-Honey fungus	"
P	1959	15'03	4 trunks	Ash	Ancient bank	"

Old Wraxall Court Estate

Pri/Open	No.	Size	Feature	Type	Location	Map Ref.
P	1789	16'03	20' at 5'	Lime	Wood east of public foot path	72/48
P	1790	14'03		Lime	Ham Farm to top of West Hill	"
P	1957	M/T		Yew	West Hill	"
P	1958	M/T		Yew	Top End	"

Wraxall   Failand House

Pri/Open	No.	Size	Feature	Type	Location	Map Ref.
P	987	M/T		Lime	Woods	73/51
P	988	17'05		Lime	"	"
P	989	18'06		Wellingtonia	"	"
P	990	15'08		Willow	"	"
P	1990	14'03		Oak	Woods, south east	"
P	1991	1?'06		Willow	"	"
P	1992	16'06		Lime	Garden	"
P	1993	15'00		Beech	Garden	"
P	*	*	Under 14'00	Gingko	" - planted 1744 by Lord Braithwaite	

Wraxall — Failand Hill House

Pri/Open	No.	Size	Feature	Type	Location	Map Ref.
P	659	28'00		Wellingtonia	House grounds	72/51
P	660	20'06		Wellingtonia	"	"
P	661	14'10		Wellingtonia	"	"
P	662	14'00		Beech	"	"

Wraxall — Show Ground Area

Pri/Open	No.	Size	Feature	Type	Location	Map Ref.
O	2094	19'06		Oak	First Field	70.71/49.50
O	2095	15'00	Topped	Oak	"	"
O	2096	14'04		Oak	"	"
O	2097	14'04		Oak	"	"
O	2098	14'00		Oak	Second Field	"
O	2099	14'00		Oak	" , Hill	"
O	2100	W/O	M/T	Alder	Bathing Pool Brook	"

Wraxall — Tyntesfield House (no public access)

Pri/Open	No.	Size	Feature	Type	Location	Map Ref.
P	891	21'02		Beech	Driveway, right hand side	70-72/49-51
P	892	14'00		Beech	"	"
P	893	18'08		Oak	"	"
P	894	16'08		Oak	"	"
P	895	U/O		Lime	"	"
P	896	U/O	7 trunks	Cypress	Driveway, right hand side, stables entrance	"
P	897	14'06		Holm/Turkey Oak	"	"
P	898	26'04		Wellingtonia	Driveway, right hand side	"
P	899	15'06		Cedar	"	"
P	900	14'01		Sweet Chestnut	Driveway, right hand side, estate office entrance	"
P	901	14'09		Sweet Chestnut	"	"
P	902	16'05		Sweet Chestnut	"	"
P	903	15'09		Sweet Chestnut	"	"
P	904	14'09		Sweet Chestnut	"	"
P	905	17'04		Maple	Driveway, left hand side	"
P	906	17'05		Maple	"	"
P	907	14'02		Maple	"	"
P	908	16'04		Willow	Front lawn, right hand side	"
P	909	M/T		Willow	"	"

Wraxall

Tyntesfield House (no public access)

Pri/Open	No.	Size	Feature	Type	Location	Map Ref.
P	910	M/T		Cypress	Right hand side lawn	70-72/49-51
P	911	M/T		Cypress	"	"
P	912	19'04		Cedar	"	"
P	913	17'02		Sweet Chestnut	"	"
P	914	14'02	6 trunks	Sycamore	"	"
P	915	15'00		Yew	Rose garden	"
P	916	18'07		Coast Redwood	"	"
P	917	M/T		Cypress	Rose Garden	"
P	918	M/T		Cypress	"	"
P	921	16'03		Oak	Oak Park below house, by gate (no public access)	"
P	922	19'00		Oak	Oak Park below house, right hand side	
P	923	14'08		Oak	"	"
P	924	14'07		Cedar	"	"
P	925	21'07		Wellingtonia	"	"
P	926	17'04		Cedar	Oak Park below house, top right hand side	"
P	927	14'04		Oak	"	"
P	928	16'09		Sweet Chestnut	Oak Park below house, centre	"
P	929	16'10		Oak	")	"
P	930	14'06		Oak	")	"
P	931	18'08		Oak	") 4 together	"
P	932	15'09		Oak	")	"
P	933	18'06		Oak	Oak Park below house, centre	"
P	934	15'06		Oak	Oak Park below house, left hand side	"
P	936	14'06		Lime	Rape field left of Lower Lodge, Lime avenue	"
P	937	15'04		Lime	"	"
P	938	15'00		Lime	"	"
P	939	18'05		Beech	Lane - Wraxall North to Home Farm, left side	"
P	940	14'00		Beech	"	"
P	941	14'00	Split	Beech	"	"
P	942	17'06		Beech	" right side	
P	950	14'10		Oak	Rape field right of lower house	"
P	951	15'09		Sweet Chestnut	Rape field middle of lower house	"
P	952	17'05		Sweet Chestnut	"	"
P	953	15'02		Sweet Chestnut	"	"
P	954	14'09		Oak	Rape field left of lower house	"
P	955	14'04		Oak	"	"
P	956	16'01		Lime	Grass, Oak Park, right of drive, left side (no public access)	"
P	957	14'10	Beech		"	"
P	958	18'08	Oak		"	"
P	969	19'00		Lime	" middle	"
P	970	18'00		Oak	" middle	"

Wraxall

Tyntesfield Grounds

Pri/Open	No.	Size	Feature	Type	Location	Map Ref.
P	971	17'06		Beech	Grass, Oak Park, right of drive, left side (no public access)	70-72/49-51
P	972	15'08		Oak	"	bottom "
P	973	16'06		Oak	"	right side "
P	974	16'00		Oak	"	left side "
P	975	14'09		Beech	"	middle "
P	976	17'09		Oak	"	middle "
P	977	18'00		Oak	"	left side "
P	978	15'07		Oak	"	bottom "
P	979	14'03		Oak	"	middle "
P	980	22'00		Oak	"	middle "
P	981	20'07		Oak	"	middle "
P	982	14'00		Oak	"	middle "
P	983	15'05		Oak	"	top "
P	943	14'04		Lime	Main drive above house (no public access)	"
P	944	U/O		Lime	"	"
P	945	U/O		Lime	"	"
P	946	U/O		Lime	"	"
P	947	U/O		Lime	"	"
P	948	14'09	80' tall	Lime	"	"
P	949	14'00		Lime	"	"
P	959	16'03		Beech	Fields below Sidelands Wood	"
P	960	16'00		Lime	"	"
P	961	14'00		Sweet Chestnut	"	"
P	962	14'00		Sweet Chestnut	"	"
O	1253	14'00		Beech	Sidelands Wood	"
O	1254	14'00		Beech	"	"
O	1255	M/T		Yew	"	"
O	1256	M/T		Sycamore	"	"
			Note:	10+ Beech over 10' in Sidelands Wood		
P	1783	M/T	Old Stool	Ash	Trucklewood	"
P	1784	M/T		Ash	"	"
P	1785	M/T		Beech	"	"
P	1786	M/T		Beech	"	"
P	1787	14'03		Oak	"	"

Wraxall

Tyntesfield Plantation

Pri/Open	No.	Size	Feature	Type	Location	Map Ref. 70.71.72/49.50.51
P	1210	14'06	*Twin trunk*	Lime	Top drive	"
P	1211	15'06		Yew	Belmont Coombe	"
P	1212	14'09		Yew	"	"
P	1213	17'00	*Dead*	Oak	"	"
P	1214	M/T		Yew	"	"
P	1215	M/T		Yew	"	"
P	1216	14'00	*25' base, old pollard*	Oak	Woods	
P	1217	18'07		Plane	Lower drive	"
P	1218	17'05	M/T	Lime	"	"
P	1219	17'03		Cedar	"	"
P	1220	17'09	*3 trunk*	Oak	Near 1778 old stone	"
P	1221	18'00	*Pollard*	Oak	Middle drive	"
P	1222	15'10	"	Oak	"	"
P	1223	15'04	"	Oak	" *next to Yew*	"
P	1224	M/T		Yew	"	"
P	1225	U/O	*Pollard*	Oak	"	"
P	1226	14'00		Beech	"	"
P	1227	14'02		Beech	"	"
P	1228	14'10		Beech	"	"
P	1229	M/T		Yew	"	"
P	1230	14'03	*Two branches collapsed*	Beech	"	"
P	1231	17'05	*20'+at 5' up decayed*	Yew	"	"
P	1232	16'08		Beech	Bottom drive	"
P	1233	18'03	*Pollard*	Oak	"	"
P	1234	17'09	"	Oak	"	"
P	1235	20'00	"	Oak	"	"
P	1236	U/O		Beech	Middle drive	
P	1237	U/O		Beech	"	"
P	1238	14'07		Beech	"	"
P	1239	15'00		Beech	Top drive	"
P	1240	16'07	Huge	Beech	Top drive, next to ruin	"

Wraxall

Downs School Area

Pri/Open	No.	Size	Feature	Type	Location		Map Ref.
P	513	16'03		Copper Beech	Downs School grounds		73/49
P	514	16'00		Oak	"		"
P	515	14'10		Yew	"		"
P	516	14'01		Oak	Fields south east of school, in a copse		"
P	517	16'04		Oak	"	by fence	"
P	518	C/O		Oak	"	by fence	"
P	1173	C/O		Oak	"	by fence	"
P	1174	C/O		Oak	"	by fence	"
P	1175	14'02		Beech	"	by fence	"
P	1176	16'00		Lime	"	by fence	"
		L shaped 10'6 bough, huge - 25' at 10' up					
P	1177	14'07		Sycamore	Fields south west of school		"
P	1178	15'07		Oak	"		"
P	1179	15'08	*Huge root base*	Sycamore	"		"
P	1180	17'04		Luncombe Oak	"		"
P	1181	18'02		Luncombe Oak	"		"
P	1182	14'00		Luncombe Oak	"		"
P	1183	18'06	*5 trunks, base measure*	Sycamore	Breach Woods		"
P	1184	15'04	*4 trunks, base measure*	Ash	"		"
P	1185	14'07	*4 trunks, base measure*	Ash	"		"
P	1186	19'02	*10 trunks, base measure*	Sweet Chestnut	"		"
P	1187	17'03	*17'03 at 20'*	Beech	"		"
P	1188	16'00	*3 trunks, base measure*	Sweet Chestnut	"		"
P	1189	M/T	*80'+ tall*	Lime	"		"
P	1190	14'00	M/T	Sycamore	Breach Woods		"
P	1191	14'08	*Single trunk*	Sycamore	Charlton Farm Fields		"
P	1192	18'05		Luncombe Oak	East of drive		"
P	1193	16'06		Oak	"		"
P	1194	15'10		Beech	"		"
P	119S	14'00	*Huge base*	Ash	West of drive		"

Wrington

Largest Cedar in North Somerset, 25'00 (ref. 2107). Large Sycamore, public foot path, 21'05 (ref. 191). One of the largest Cypress in North Somerset, 20' (ref. 14). 18'02 single trunk Ash (ref. 783) at entrance to North Field House. Sycamore, 17'09 (ref. 1502) at St Katherines farm. This tree is a huge, spreading single trunk probably the best perfect example of a large Sycamore anywhere that I have seen. Largest Alder, 24'08 (ref. 1610) single trunk (whereabouts unavailable as the area is private and there is no access for the general public)

On Foot   Corporation Woods - River walk, Congresbury - Goblin Combe Wrington Warren

In the car   See Congresbury

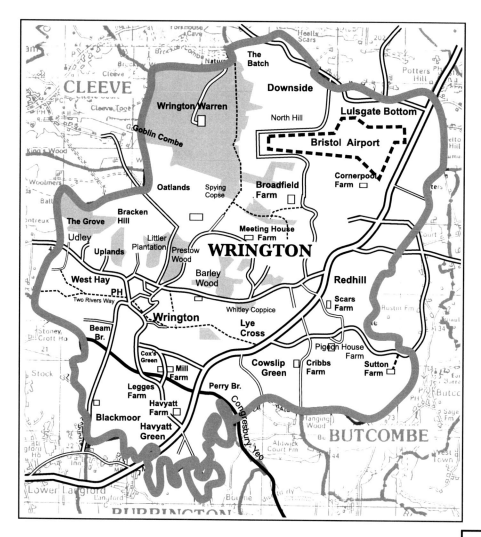

Beech – Ref. 73, 16'06
◁ *Donkey Field, Uphill, W-s-M*
'Lauren Smith and her Daddy'

⋏
Copper Beech – Ref. 513, 16'03
Downs School, Wraxall

Sweet Chestnut– Ref. 151, 21'02
◁ *Above Ashton Court House*
to the left.

Wrington

Pri/Open	No.	Size	Feature	Type	Location	Map Ref.
P	157	23'02	*Pollard*	Oak	Field below Long Lane	62/48
P	86	16'00	"	Oak	"	"
O	71	16'01		Wellingtonia	Alburys	63/46
P	778	16'00	*Coppice*	Ash	South Broadfleld Farm	63/49
P	779	14'08	*Split trunk*	Ash	" hedgerow	"
P	780	14'00	*6 trunks*	Field Maple	" hedgerow	"
P	781	18'08	*3 trunks,*	Field Maple	" hedgerow	"
P	782	14'01		Ash	" near public footpath stile	"
P	783	18'02	*Single trunk*	Ash	North Hill House downside	65/50
P	784	21'00	*Split trunk*	Lime	"	"
O	1313	M/T	*Layered*	Lime	Wrington Hill Farm Road, public footpath	64/47
P	1438	14'01		Cypress	Cowslip Green House	61/48
P	1439	15'07	*Mistletoe*	Willow	Field, Cowslip Green	"
P	1502	17'09	*Huge, spreading*	Sycamore	St Katherines Farm, Lulsgate Bottom *(Largest Sycamore in North Somerset)*	65/50
O	310	18'03		Oak	Havyatts Green, A38	61/47
P	1559	16'03	*Triple trunk*	Horse Chestnut	Booklodge Farm	"
P	232	14'02		Sweet Chestnut	The Grove	63/46
O	191	21'05	*Coppice*	Sycamore	The Grove, public footpath	"
P	1283	15'04		Beech	Woods near The Grove	"
P	1284	14'06	*Single trunk*	Lime	"	"
P	1285	17'06	*Split*	Oak	"	"
P	146	20'00		Cypress	Uplands House	"
P	109	17'00		Oak	"	"
P	91	16'06		Sweet Chestnut	"	"
P	63	15'04		Beech	"	"
P	1258	M/T		Sycamore	Grove/Upland Wood	"
P	1259	19'00	*Base measure*	Lime	"	"
P	1260	18'00	*Single trunk*	Lime	"	"
P	1261	M/T	*Stool*	Ash	"	"
P	1262	M/T		Ash	"	"
P	1263	M/T		Lime	"	"
P	1264	M/T		Lime	"	"
P	1697	M/T	*Triple trunk*	Ash	Below Scars Wood	62/50
P	1698	M/T	*Layered*	Ash	Above Redhill Wood	64/50
P	1699	M/T		Ash	High Wood	"
P	1700	M/T		Ash	"	"

Wrington

Pri/Open	No.	Size	Feature	Type	Location	Map Ref.
P	1701	M/T		Ash	High Wood	64/50
P	1702	M/T		Ash	"	"
P	1703	M/T		Field Maple	"	"
P	1598	W/O	Multi trunk	Alder	East of Perry Bridge, River Yeo, A38	61/48
P	1599	W/O		Alder	"	"
P	1600	W/O		Alder	"	"
P	1601	W/O		Alder	"	"
P	1602	W/O		Alder	"	"
P	1603	W/O		Alder	"	"
P	1604	W/O		Alder	"	"
P	1605	W/O		Alder	"	"
P	1606	W/O		Alder	"	"
P	1607	M/T	Coppice	Hazel	"	"
P	1608	16'00	"	Sycamore	"	"
P	1609	W/O	"	Sycamore	East of Perry Bridge, River Yeo, A38	61/48
P	1610	24'08	Split trunk	Alder	"	"
P	1611	W/O	Trunk bridge	Willow	"	"
P	1612	15'04	Single trunk	Willow	"	"
P	1613	15'10		Ash	"	"
P	1614	15'07		Willow	Rickford Stream, Perry Bridge south to public footpath	"
P	1615	M/T		Willow	"	"
P	1617	W/O		Alder	"	"
P	1618	W/O		Alder	"	"
P	1619	W/O		Alder	"	"
P	1620	W/O		Alder	"	"
P	1621	W/O		Alder	"	"
P	1622	M/T	6 trunks	Willow	Rickford Stream, PFP to Burrington Parish Boundary	"
P	1623	W/O		Alder	"	"
P	1624	W/O		Alder	"	"
P	1625	W/O		Alder	"	"
O	1672	W/O		Alder	River Yeo, Congresbury Parish Boundary to Beam Bridge	62/46
O	1673	W/O		Alder	"	"
O	1674	W/O		Alder	"	"
O	1675	W/O		Alder	"	"
O	1676	W/O		Alder	"	"
O	1677	W/O		Alder	"	"
O	1678	W/O		Alder	"	"
O	1679	W/O		Alder	"	"

Wrington

Pri/Open	No.	Size	Feature	Type	Location	Map Ref.
O	1680	W/O	*3 trunks*	Willow	River Yeo, Congresbury Parish Boundary to Beam Bridge	62/46
O	1681	W/O		Willow	"	"
O	1682	W/O		Sycamore	"	"
P	1683	W/O		Alder	Beam Bridge to Havyatts Road, River Yeo	61/47
P	1684	W/O		Alder		"
P	1685	W/O		Alder		"
P	1686	W/O		Willow	"	"
O	1687	W/O		Alder	Beam Bridge to Havyatts Road Mill Stream, River Yeo	61/47
O	1688	W/O		Alder		"
O	1689	W/O		Alder	"	"
O	1690	W/O		Alder	"	"
O	1691	W/O		Alder	"	"
P	1765	W/O		Ash	River Yeo Old River, Perry Bridge to Mill Lane	"
P	1766	W/O		Ash	"	"
P	1767	W/O		Ash	"	"
P	1768	W/O		Ash	"	"
P	1769	W/O		Alder	"	"
P	1770	W/O		Alder	"	"
P	1771	W/O		Alder	"	"
P	1772	W/O		Alder	"	"
P	1773	W/O		Alder	"	"
P	1774	W/O	*Huge*	Sycamore	"	"
P	1775	W/O		Oak	"	"
P	1776	W/O		Alder	River Yeo, Mill Lane to Coxes Green, next to waterfall	62/47
P	1777	W/O	*Very large trunk, small tree*	Alder	"	"
O	2088	20'02		Oak	Field, Wood Road public footpath	63/43
O	2089	18'01		Oak	Near pond, Wood Road public footpath	"
O	2090	16'09		Oak	Field, Wood Road public footpath	"
O	2091	14'00	*Top blown off*	Oak	West Hay (Lamas in field)	"
O	2092	16'02	*Single trunk*	Willow	Court Farm, south of public footpath	"
P	2107	25'00	*Largest Cedar in N. Somerset*	Cedar	Cedar House, Wrington	63/47

Yatton

19'01 Wellingtonia (ref. 664) at Cadbury Hill Nature Reserve.

In the Car	See Congresbury
On Foot	Cadbury Hill Nature Reserve
	Kings Wood, Cleeve – Claverham

Claverham

Very large Horse Chestnut 16'10 (ref. 187) right opposite the childrens school. If you go there in Autumn you can see the children collecting conkers. They seem to enjoy themselves, as do their parents.

In the Car	See Cleeve
On Foot	See Cleeve

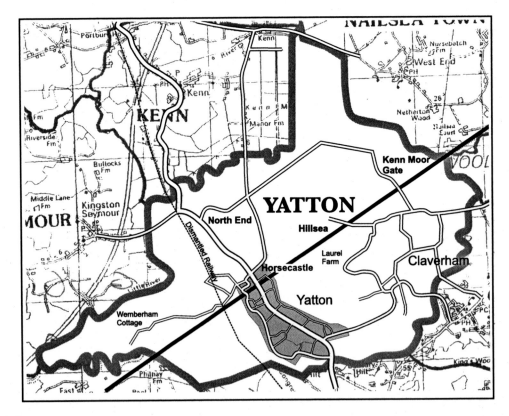

"Take the children and grandchildren safely on their bikes to Congresbury via the Old Strawberry Line"

Yatton

Pri/Open	No.	Size	Feature	Type	Location	Map Ref.
O	664	19'01		Wellingtonia	Cadbury Hill Nature Reserve	65/44
O	663	17'00	*Swing*	Oak	"	"
O	1001	14'02		Oak	"	"
O	1002	W/O	*Pollard*	Willow	Rhyne, Claverham Drove	66/99
O	1003	W/O	"	Willow	"	"
O	1004	W/O	"	Willow	"	"
O	1005	W/O	"	Willow	"	"
O	1006	W/O	"	Willow	"	"
O	187	16'10		Horse Chestnut	Bishops Road opposite Claverham School	"

❑ ❑ ❑ ❑ ❑ ❑ ❑

Answers to Twelve Trees to Find

1. 16'10 Horse Chestnut (ref. 187), Claverham School
2. 18'10 Cedar (ref. 309) Glebe Close
3. 27'6 Yew (ref. 472), Abbots Leigh Churchyard
4. 18'1 Oak (ref. 815), Portishead Lake car park
5. 16'6 Beech (ref. 73), Uphill donkey field.
6. 15'01 Wellingtonia, cut down and made in to a sculpture at Churchill crossroads traffic lights.
7. 15'06 (ref. 763) Willow, Bleadon Hill
8. 17'04 (ref. 1780) Wellingtonia on the old Strawberry Line at Sandford
9. 26'6 Oak (ref. 254) at Brockley Woods
10. 16'02 Holm Oak (ref. 1932) in Clevedon Court Woods
11. 3 5 Wellingtonias, Ashton Hill Plantation, Long Ashton
12. 6 Wellingtonias. Ashton Court House, Ashton Court Estate, Long Ashton

FOUND THEM ALL – WELL DONE
YOU ARE NOW AN ACCOMPLISHED TREE-HUNTER

Trees I have discovered

Pri/Open	Size	Features	Type	Location	Map Ref.